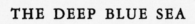
THE DEEP BLUE SEA

THE
DEEP
BLUE
SEA

by TERENCE RATTIGAN

RANDOM HOUSE
NEW YORK

FIRST PRINTING

Photograph on binding by Vandamm

The Deep Blue Sea was originally performed in London in March, 1952, and was first produced in New York by Alfred de Liagre and John C. Wilson at the Morosco Theatre on the night of November 5, 1952, with the following cast:

[In Order of Appearance]

HESTER COLLYER	*Margaret Sullavan*
MRS. ELTON	*Betty Sinclair*
PHILIP WELCH	*John Merivale*
ANN WELCH	*Stella Andrew*
MR. MILLER	*Herbert Berghof*
WILLIAM COLLYER	*Alan Webb*
FREDERICK PAGE	*James Hanley*
JACKIE JACKSON	*Felix Deebank*

Direction by Frith Banbury

Setting and Lighting supervised by Charles Elson

SCENES

ACT ONE: Morning

ACT TWO: Afternoon

ACT THREE: Evening

The action passes during the course of a day in September in the sitting room of a furnished flat in the northwest of London.

ACT ONE

ACT ONE

The sitting room of a furnished flat in the northwest of London. It is a big room for it is on the second floor of a large and gloomy Victorian mansion, converted to flats after World War I, but it has an air of dinginess, even of squalor, heightened by the fact that it has, like its immediate badly blitzed neighborhood, so obviously "come down in the world."

There is a door backstage leading to the first-floor landing of the house, and another, downstage, leading into the bedroom. There is another small door, to the right of landing door evidently put in when the house was converted and which gives access to a tiny kitchen.

There is a window at right, curtained at the moment, and in the left wall is a fireplace, originally designed for coal, but now occupied by a gas fire. On the floor in front of this, dimly seen in the darkened room, lies HESTER COLLYER, *with her head covered by a rug, very close to the unlit stove.*

At rise, there is a knocking at the door, increasing in volume, coincident with the rise of the curtain. There is a pause, then another knock, louder this time. Another pause, and the doorbell sounds with an air of urgency. A woman (MRS. ELTON *) calls from off-stage.*

3

MRS. ELTON
(*Off-stage*)

Mrs. Page! (*Knock*) Mr. Page! I think it's coming from here. I'd better use the passkey.

(*Another voice* (ANN WELCH'S) *can be heard off stage.*)

ANN

What's the matter?

(PHILIP WELCH, *Ann's husband, answers.*)

PHILIP
(*Off-stage*)

Escape of gas, darling. Don't light a match, will you?

(*There is the sound of a key in the lock, and the door opens, revealing* MRS. ELTON *on the threshold. She is caretaker-housekeeper to the flats, and is in the middle fifties. Behind her is* PHILIP WELCH, *aged about twenty-four and, from his clothes, an office worker.*)

MRS. ELTON

Phew! It's here all right. They must have left something on.

(*She comes into the flat.*)

PHILIP

Careful, Mrs. Elton. Put something over your mouth—

4

MRS. ELTON

Oh, it's not as bad as that. Wicked waste. (*She reaches the window, draws the curtains briskly and flings up the window*) Someone'll blow this whole house up one of these days—that's what'll happen—

> (*While muttering she has been adjusting the drapes and window. Meanwhile* PHILIP *has taken a step or two inside the room, and now sees the prostrate* HESTER *by the fire.*)

PHILIP

My God! (*He calls urgently*) Mrs. Elton.

MRS. ELTON

What's the matter?

PHILIP

Mrs. Elton! Quick. Get a doctor or someone—

> (*He raises* HESTER's *head away from the fire, and pulls the rug off her.*)

MRS. ELTON

Oh, heavens!

PHILIP
(*Fumbling for the gas faucet*)
Where does this thing turn off?

MRS. ELTON

Mrs. Page! Mrs. Page!! (*She takes* HESTER's *hand*) She's not dead, is she?

PHILIP

I don't know. I don't think so. (*In a panic*) This isn't turned off. I can't turn it off.

MRS. ELTON

Here! Let me! It *is* off! (*She turns the faucet both ways*) It wasn't on.

PHILIP

We must get her to the window. Better turn that chair around to face it.

(*He picks* HESTER *up bodily, and carries her to the chair.*)

MRS. ELTON

(*As she turns the armchair to face the window*)

This'll mean the police. In twenty-three years Mr. Elton and me have never had a speck of trouble in these flats, and now—Mrs. Page—of all people.

(PHILIP *lowers* HESTER *into the chair.* ANN, PHILIP'S *young wife, also an office worker, appears on the landing outside.*)

ANN

(*Calling*)

Philip? Are you in there?

PHILIP

Yes. Don't come in.

6

ANN
(*Off-stage*)

We'll be late for the office—

PHILIP

You go on. Tell them I'll get there as soon as I can.

ANN
(*Off-stage*)

Is anything wrong?

(*She comes into the room.*)

PHILIP
(*Savagely*)

I said not to come in.

ANN
(*She runs over to* HESTER)

Gas?

PHILIP

Yes.

(*Slightly surprised at his wife's composure.*)

MRS. ELTON

She's breathing.

PHILIP

Where's the nearest doctor?

7

MRS. ELTON

Dr. Brown. No—he's on his holiday. I know. Mr. Miller. I'll get him.

ANN

Mr. Miller upstairs, do you mean?

MRS. ELTON
(*On her way to the door*)

Yes.

ANN
(*Running after*)

But he's not a doctor!

MRS. ELTON
(*Running up the stairs*)

Mr. Miller! Mr. Miller!

ANN
(*Coming back to Philip*)

She's hysterical, Philip. Mr. Miller's not a doctor—

(PHILIP *has gone to gas fire,* ANN *joins him.*)

PHILIP

See this? (*He picks up a little empty bottle from the grate*) Aspirin. Empty.

ANN

Oh, Lord!

PHILIP

And here's the glass. (*He picks up glass from mantel*) She ground them in here. Look.

ANN

She must have wanted to dope herself, before the gas had any effect.

PHILIP

The gas was off. The tap was turned on, but the gas was off. It must have run out in the meter—

ANN

What do you mean?

PHILIP

They've got one of those shilling-in-the-slot affairs. The gas cuts off automatically, after a time, unless you put another shilling in.

ANN

What a bit of luck! Where's her husband?

PHILIP

I don't know. (*He opens the bedroom door and looks inside*) The bed hasn't been slept in.

ANN

We ought to get hold of him somehow.

PHILIP

Yes, but how?

9

ANN
(*Excitedly, as she goes to* HESTER)
She's opened her eyes. (PHILIP *joins* ANN *at the chair*)
Mrs. Page! Mrs. Page!

HESTER

(*Speaking in a low, thick murmur, the words barely
distinguishable*)
Finished—Freddy—finished—

PHILIP
Mrs. Page, it's all right—everything's all right, now—

HESTER
(*With a low moan*)
You—must understand—how happy—like sleep—Freddy
—sleep—forgive bad writing—poor Freddy—poor darling
Freddy—

(*She moans again, as if in a bad dream, and closes
her eyes, shaking her head.*)

ANN
Don't worry, Mrs. Page. You mustn't worry. You're among
friends—(MR. MILLER, *unshaven and in shabby dressing
gown, comes in hurriedly, followed by* MRS. ELTON. *He is
about forty and when he speaks it is possible to detect a
slight German accent. He is carrying a battered instrument
case. He goes over to the chair and pushes* ANN *and* PHILIP
rather brusquely out of the way, before kneeling down in

10

front of HESTER. *With quick deft movements he makes an obviously practiced and professional, if cursory, examination*) She came to, a moment ago, and talked. She kept on saying Freddy. And something about being happy—like sleep—

PHILIP
And then she said something about bad writing.

ANN
Forgive her bad writing, it was.

PHILIP
I didn't hear forgive. I just heard—bad writing. We found this (PHILIP *holds up the empty aspirin bottle*) on the floor.

> (MILLER *takes the bottle, glances at it, nods.* MILLER *has paid no attention to* ANN *and* PHILIP. HESTER *opens her eyes, bewildered.* MILLER *holds the aspirin bottle up before her eyes.*)

MILLER
How many? (HESTER *closes her eyes*) How many?

HESTER
(*Quite clearly*)
Twenty.

(*She closes her eyes again.*)

MILLER
(*To* MRS. ELTON)
Where's the bedroom?

MRS. ELTON

(*Hustling to open the door*)

In here.

MILLER

Help me, please. (MILLER *and* PHILIP *carry her to the door. To* ANN) Bring my case, would you please? (*He goes, with his burden, into the bedroom.* PHILIP *picks up his case and goes in after him*) A glass of warm water please, Mrs. Elton.

MRS. ELTON

Yes, straight away.

(*She comes back into the sitting room, and goes into the kitchen.*)

PHILIP

Look, darling, hadn't you better get on to the office? It's all right for me, but I don't like the idea of you being late.

(*He goes into bedroom.*)

ANN

(*As* PHILIP *returns*)

They'll understand. There's never much in on Mondays. Poor soul. I wonder what made her do it. Freddy—that's her husband, I suppose?

PHILIP

I think so, yes. I've seen his letters downstairs. Frederick Page, Esquire.

ANN

I've never liked the look of him.

PHILIP

She said "poor darling Freddy." That doesn't sound as if he'd deserted her, or anything.

ANN

Then where is he?

PHILIP

Husbands do, you know, occasionally go off on business without taking their wives.

> (MRS. ELTON *comes out of the kitchen with a glass of warm water. She crosses to the bedroom door, knocks and goes in.* ANN *goes over to her husband.*)

ANN

I wish we could help, somehow. (*She is looking at the fireplace and notices something. She goes quickly over and takes a letter off the mantelpiece*) Yes, of course.

PHILIP

What?

ANN

(*Holding up the letter*)

Suicide note.

PHILIP

Who's it addressed to?

ANN

(*Reading*)

Freddy. It's in pencil—very faint. Should we open it?

PHILIP

No. It may be wanted by the police.

ANN

The police? Oh, dear.

PHILIP

(*Unhappily*)

I suppose we ought to ring them up.

(ANN *puts the letter back on the mantelpiece.*)

ANN

It's a sordid business, isn't it, a suicide? I wonder if they think of that when they do it—police and coroners and things. I suppose we'll have to give evidence.

PHILIP

If there's an inquest, yes. But let's pray it doesn't come to that.

ANN

Attempted suicide is a crime, anyway, isn't it? People get jailed for it, don't they?

14

PHILIP

Yes.

ANN

Well, then, you mustn't ring up the police. Not yet
anyway.

PHILIP

We ought to get in touch with somebody, though. I wish
to God her husband would come. (MRS. ELTON *comes out
of the bedroom. He speaks to her*) How is she?

MRS. ELTON

He didn't say, but she's looking better. He's given her an
injection of something that made her sick. I've got to make
some black coffee. (*She goes into the kitchen, while* ANN
and PHILIP *confer*) Oh, there's some here already. I'll just
need to warm it up.

PHILIP
(*Calling after her*)

Mrs. Elton, we both think we ought to get hold of Mr.
Page. Have you any idea where he might be?

(MRS. ELTON *appears at the door with a percolator
in hand.*)

MRS. ELTON

No. I can't say I have.

PHILIP

Where does he work?

15

MRS. ELTON

I don't know that he does work—not regularly, that is. He's often here all day, I know that. I believe he's something to do with aeroplanes—or used to be, anyway.

PHILIP

Selling them?

MRS. ELTON

No. Flying them, I think. Test pilot—isn't that what they call it?

PHILIP

Yes.

MRS. ELTON

Anyway, I don't think he's doing it any more—

(*She goes back into the kitchen.*)

ANN

She must have some relations in London we could get hold of.

PHILIP

Yes. (*He goes to the kitchen door again. Calling*) Mrs. Elton, do you know if Mrs. Page has any relations in London?

(MRS. ELTON *reappears and comes in, leaving the kitchen door open.*)

16

MRS. ELTON

No. I can't say I do.

PHILIP

Can you think of any particular friend then? Haven't you
ever heard her talk about anybody?

MRS. ELTON

No. Always kept herself very much to herself, Mrs. Page.

ANN

She must have had visitors—

MRS. ELTON

Hardly ever, and they always asked for him—not for her.

PHILIP

What were their names?

MRS. ELTON

I can't remember.

PHILIP

Do try and help, Mrs. Elton. This is desperately important.

MRS. ELTON

I'm sorry, Mr. Welch. It's the shock.

PHILIP

Yes, yes, of course. But now look. Think hard. Don't you

know of anyone connected with Mrs. Page that we might get into touch with?

ANN

Lawyer—bank manager?
    (MRS. ELTON *is thinking.*)

MRS. ELTON
(*At length*)

There *is* her husband, of course—

PHILIP
(*With a hopeless gesture*)

I know—but we haven't an idea where he is—

MRS. ELTON

Oh, I don't mean—(*She looks alarmed*) No, I can't think of anyone.

    (*She turns to go back into the kitchen.*)

ANN
(*Sharply*)

Mrs. Elton. What did you mean by "There *is* her husband"?

    (MRS. ELTON *turns slowly.*)

PHILIP

Isn't Mr. Page her husband?

ANN

What's her real name?

18

MRS. ELTON

I haven't said anything.

PHILIP

Look, Mrs. Elton, if the police come, it'll all have to come out anyway. You don't need to tell us anything you don't want to; but I do think that if you know her real husband you ought to ring him up and tell him what's happened.

MRS. ELTON

I don't know her real husband. I only found out about it by accident, and I promised faithfully I'd never tell a living soul, not even Mr. Elton. It's none of his business, or mine, or anyone else's, come to that.

(*She goes into the kitchen.* PHILIP *and* ANN *exchange a glance.*)

ANN

I'm sure I'm right now, Philip, This man Page has deserted her, and she had no one to turn to. She's probably quarreled with her family, and her friends have dropped her, most likely—

(MRS. ELTON *emerges with a cup on a tray.*)

MRS. ELTON

So you think I ought to tell her husband about this?

PHILIP

Well, yes, Mrs. Elton. It seems to me the only thing to do.

MRS. ELTON

All right. You do it. I wouldn't know how. Her name is Collyer—(*Spelling it*) C O L L Y E R, and her husband's name's in the papers quite often. She showed me once. They call him Mr. Justice Collyer—so I suppose he's a judge.

ANN

William Collyer.

MRS. ELTON

That's right. Sir William Collyer.

(*She goes into the bedroom.*)

PHILIP
(*Awed*)

Gosh!

ANN

Do you think you dare, Philip?

PHILIP

I don't see why not.

(*He has grasped a telephone book and is looking through it.*)

ANN
(*In a panic*)

Whatever you do, don't tell him you work for the Home Office.

20

PHILIP

(*He looks at his watch*)

Quarter past nine. We ought to get him at his home. Here
we are—Collyer—William—(*He dials a number.* ANN *waits
by his side, alarmed and excited*) Hullo. Could I speak to
Sir William Collyer, please? . . . No, I'd rather not give my
name. Just tell him that it's very urgent indeed, and that it
concerns his wife—His wife—Yes. I'll wait. (*He takes* ANN's
*hand and presses it affectionately. He is evidently rather en-
joying his strong male act and knows that he is impressing*
ANN) Hullo! Sir William Collyer? I'm afraid I have some
serious news for you. Your wife has been concerned in—in an
accident. It's rather difficult to tell you that on the telephone
—Well, If you insist. Gas poisoning, and an overdose of
drugs—No, but very ill—No. She doesn't know I'm tele-
phoning. He's not here—27 Weybridge Villas, Ladbroke
Grove—Yes. Flat Number Three, one flight up—You'll find
the front door open. Yes. There's a doctor—that's to say, she's
being given medical attention now. (*He rings off*) He's coming straight round.

ANN

Did he seem upset?

PHILIP

It was rather difficult to tell. He asked if Page was here.
(MRS. ELTON *comes out of the bedroom*) I've rung him up,
Mrs. Elton. He's coming round.

21

MRS. ELTON
(*Slowly*)

I only hope we've done the right thing.

ANN

I think we have.

PHILIP

How is she?

MRS. ELTON

Sitting up now. Drank her coffee quite peacefully. Of course, still very weak.

ANN

Don't you think we ought to get her a proper doctor?

MRS. ELTON

I've got far more faith in Mr. Miller than in any proper doctor, thank you very much. He's done a sight more for Mr. Elton than any of those Harley Street specialists ever did—five guineas or no five guineas.

PHILIP

How is—Mr. Elton?

MRS. ELTON

He'd be much better if it weren't for this damp weather. Shocking bad for arthritis, it's been. I've been fixing his pillows all night long. (*She goes to the door*) Well, I haven't started on my hall yet. Give me a shout if I'm wanted, will you? (PHILIP *and* ANN *nod.* MILLER *comes out of the bedroom*) Will you be wanting me for anything more?

MILLER

No, Mrs. Elton.

MRS. ELTON

I'll leave this door on the latch.

(*She goes out.*)

MILLER

(*To* PHILIP)

Have you a cigarette?

PHILIP

Yes, indeed. (*He brings out a small packet.* MILLER *takes a cigarette and lights it*) My name is Welch. I live upstairs in Five. This is my wife.

(MILLER *nods to* ANN.)

MILLER

Are you friends of hers?

ANN

No. My husband found Mrs. Page this morning and we were just waiting around to see if there's anything we can do.

MILLER

There is nothing you can do.

ANN

(*Appalled*)

You don't mean she's dying?

MILLER

A hundred grains of aspirin are hardly enough to kill a woman of her age, and the symptoms of gas poisoning are very slight—

PHILIP

That's because the gas gave out at the meter?

MILLER

Yes. She couldn't have bungled it worse, could she? I'm going back to my breakfast and I'm sure there is no reason whatever for your staying here any longer. Good morning.

ANN

But is she really all right?

MILLER

I've told you. After twenty-four hours in bed she will be completely recovered.

ANN

Yes—her body. But what about her mind?

24

MILLER

(*Amused*)

You make that distinction? Her mind is perfectly sound. There is no trace whatever of any psychotic symptoms which might justify a certificate of insanity.

ANN

Yes, but she did try to kill herself, didn't she?

MILLER

It would seem so.

ANN

Well, what made her do that?

MILLER

(*After a slight pause*)

She wanted to die, I suppose.

PHILIP

But mightn't she try to do it again, Doctor?

MILLER

I'm not a doctor.

PHILIP

No. Don't you think she might try to do it again?

MILLER

I'm not a prophet either. In fact, I make a fairly respectable living out of other peoples's pretensions to prophecy. Still, if you want me to place a bet for once, I would say that she probably will try again, and try again very soon.

ANN
(*Indignantly*)

But isn't there anything we can do about it?

MILLER

No.
(*He goes out.*)

PHILIP

Well, there's a callous swine, for you.

ANN

He's phony, that man. I'm certain he is. He was just trying to impress us with all that stuff about psychoses and things. Of course she needs looking after. (*The bedroom door opens and* HESTER *comes out. She is in a dressing gown, but has tidied her hair, and put on make-up. Now that we see her under more normal circumstances we find that she is in the middle thirties with a thoughtful, remote face that has no pretensions to great beauty*) Ought you to be out of bed?

HESTER

I came for a cigarette. There were some here last night, I think.

PHILIP

Have one of these.

(*He extends his packet.*)

HESTER

No, thank you. I won't smoke yours. I know I brought a packet in with me.

PHILIP

(*Going to table*)

There they are. Let me.

HESTER

Thank you. (*He lights one for her*) You're Mr. Welch, aren't you? We met downstairs once, do you remember?

PHILIP

Yes, that's right.

HESTER

And is this Mrs. Welch?

ANN

Yes.

HESTER

How do you do? Sorry. Do you mind if I sit down? I'm still feeling a little strange.

(*She sits down.*)

ANN

Don't you think you ought to go back to bed?

HESTER

No. I feel much better sitting up, thank you.

PHILIP

You've been very ill, you know.

HESTER

Oh, no. Just a bit dopey, that's all. I'm terribly sorry for all the trouble I've caused—

PHILIP AND ANN
(*Murmuring*)

That's quite all right.

HESTER

Silly accident, wasn't it? I don't know how it could possibly have happened. I'd gone to a cinema, by myself. I came back here and I remember thinking it was a bit chilly and I turned on the gas fire to light it, after that, as they say in novels, I knew no more. I couldn't find the matches, I suppose, and the fumes must have put me out—

ANN
(*Rather crossly*)

It was lucky for you that you didn't put a shilling in the meter first.

28

HESTER

The meter?

PHILIP

Yes. The gas cut off automatically.

HESTER

Oh. That's what happened, is it? (*After a pause*) Yes.
That was lucky.

(*She leans back in the chair and closes her eyes.*)

ANN

Are you sure you're feeling all right?

HESTER

(*Opening her eyes*)
Perfectly all right, thank you.

ANN

Don't you think you ought to see a proper doctor?

HESTER

Haven't I just seen a proper doctor?

ANN

No. He's just an amateur. A bookie, or something.

HESTER

A strange hobby for a bookie. He seemed very efficient.
Horribly efficient. Look, I'm sure I'm keeping you both, and
there's really no need to stay. It's been very kind of you.

PHILIP

Well—(*He looks at* ANN *for support*) The fact is I have something to tell you.

(HESTER'S *eyes are wandering over the room.* ANN *is watching her.*)

ANN

Are you looking for something?

HESTER

Yes. I think I left a letter lying around somewhere.

(ANN *goes to the mantelpiece and takes the letter from behind the clock.*)

ANN

Is this it?

(*She hands it to her.*)

HESTER

(*Gazing at it casually*)

Yes, that's the one. (*She slips it into her dressing-gown pocket. Politely to* PHILIP) You were going to tell me something, Mr. Welch.

PHILIP

You may be very angry with me.

HESTER

I hope not.

PHILIP

I hope not, too. When we found you this morning you seemed—very ill—almost at death's door, in fact. (HESTER *glances at the fireplace, but says nothing.* PHILIP *continues after a pause*) Well, Mr. Page was away, and we didn't know where to get hold of him—

HESTER

You should have asked me. He's at the King's Head Hotel, at Sunningdale.

ANN

(*Quickly*)

Are you expecting him back this morning?

HESTER

No, I think he's playing golf. (*Smiling*) I'm a golf widow, you know, Mrs. Welch. Every week-end I'm deserted. It's shocking. (*to* PHILIP) Yes, go on, Mr. Welch.

PHILIP

(*Desperately*)

Well, I felt it my duty to get in touch with someone. We didn't know where your parents lived—

HESTER

No. They're both dead anyway.

31

PHILIP

Or any of your friends. So I'm afraid I took it on myself to ring up—Sir William Collyer.

(*There is a pause.*)

HESTER

What did you tell him?

PHILIP

That there'd been an accident.

HESTER

Did you give him this address?

PHILIP

Yes. He's coming round.

HESTER

How soon?

PHILIP

He said, at once. (HESTER *looks at the bedroom door, as if meditating whether she has time for flight*) I'm sorry if I've done wrong. I couldn't know, you see.

HESTER

No, you couldn't.

THE DEEP BLUE SEA

ANN
(*Loyally*)

It was mainly my responsibility, Lady Collyer. I told Philip
he ought to ring up.

HESTER
(*Interrupting*)

Yes, I see. Do you mind not using that name?

ANN

I'm sorry.

HESTER

It was Mrs. Elton who told you?

PHILIP

She slipped it out by accident. I may say your secret is
absolutely safe with both Ann and myself.

HESTER
(*With a faint smile*)

My guilty secret? That's very kind of you.

PHILIP
(*Stiffly*)

Well, I think we must be going. Come along, Ann.

(ANN *and* PHILIP *go to the door.*)

HESTER

Good-bye. You've been very kind and I'm grateful.

PHILIP

There's no need. Let me know if there's anything I can do, won't you?

HESTER

There is something you can do. Don't breathe a word of this stupid—accident—to anyone—to anyone else, that is.

PHILIP

I won't.

HESTER

Do you know my—do you know Freddy Page?

PHILIP

No.

HESTER

If ever you should meet him you will, above all, be particularly careful not to mention anything of this to him, won't you? It might—it might alarm him—quite needlessly.

ANN

We won't say a word—either of us.

HESTER

Thank you. Good-bye.

PHILIP

Good-bye.

ANN

Good-bye—Mrs. Page.
(*She follows* PHILIP *out.* HESTER, *at the door, calls:*)

HESTER

Mrs. Elton! Mrs. Elton!

MRS. ELTON
(*Off-stage*)

Coming, dear. (MRS. ELTON *comes in, leaving the door ajar*) You're up. I'm sure you shouldn't be.

HESTER

Mrs. Elton, if Sir William Collyer comes, I don't want to see him.

MRS. ELTON

I'm sorry about that. They got it out of me—

HESTER

Yes. I know.

MRS. ELTON

What shall I tell him?

HESTER

Anything you like—provided I don't have to see him.

MRS. ELTON

Yes, dear. I understand. Would you like me to make you some more coffee?

HESTER

No, thank you, Mrs. Elton. There's nothing I want at all.

MRS. ELTON

When's Mr. Page coming home?

HESTER

I don't know. Sometime this evening, I expect.

MRS. ELTON

If you like, I'll come and sit with you, until then. I've just got to finish my work—

HESTER

It's very kind of you, Mrs. Elton, but I shall be perfectly all right alone.

MRS. ELTON
(*Doubtfully*)

Will you, dear? Are you sure?

HESTER

Yes. You can trust me.

MRS. ELTON

Oh, I didn't mean that—

HESTER
(*Gently*)

Didn't you?

MRS. ELTON

(*Angrily*)

Whatever possessed you to do a dreadful thing like that?

(*Pause.*)

HESTER

(*Lying back with her eyes closed*)

The devil, I suppose.

MRS. ELTON

I should just think it was. Are you a Catholic?

HESTER

(*Sleepily*)

No. I didn't mean that kind of devil. Or is it the same kind? Anyway when you're between any kind of devil and the deep blue sea, the deep blue sea sometimes looks very inviting. It did last night.

MRS. ELTON

I can't make you out. You're not a wicked woman—and yet what you did last night was wicked—wicked and cruel. Now supposing it had been Mr. Page and not you that we'd found lying there this morning, how would *you* have felt?

HESTER

Very, very surprised.

MRS. ELTON

Nothing more?

HESTER

Oh, yes. A lot more. A whole universe more. (*With a faint smile*) But he's not lying there, Mrs. Elton. He's playing golf. (*Pause.* MRS. ELTON *is looking at her puzzled*) And when he comes back from golf, he must know nothing of what happened last night. Do you understand, Mrs. Elton? Nothing.

MRS. ELTON

If that's the way you want it.

HESTER

That's the way I want it.

(*Pause.*)

MRS. ELTON

It's not money, is it, dear?

HESTER

No. It's not money.

MRS. ELTON

Because if it is, I was going to say—about this flat—

HESTER

It's very kind of you, Mrs. Elton, and I'm deeply grateful. But I couldn't possibly accept it. I know we owe you a month's rent—but it will be paid, I promise you, in a day or two. As a matter of fact, I've got someone who's very interested in those two pictures there.

(*She points to two pictures on the wall.*)

MRS. ELTON
(*Politely*)

Oh, yes. Very clever. How much would you get for a thing like that?

HESTER

Well, for the two I'm asking twenty-five pounds.

MRS. ELTON

Are you, really? Well, I never. (*After a slight pause*) Excuse me for asking you, won't you—but is Mr. Page in a job just now?

HESTER

Not exactly. Not at the moment. But—he has interests in the city, you know.

MRS. ELTON
(*Who has evidently heard this one before*)

Oh, yes? Well, perhaps he'll get himself something steady soon. It shouldn't be too hard these days—

(COLLYER, *a forceful-looking figure in the middle forties, dressed in short morning coat and striped trousers, stands on the threshold.*)

COLLYER

Mrs. Page?

MRS. ELTON

I'm sorry, sir— (COLLYER *and* HESTER *stare at each other without speaking*) Mrs. Page is too ill to—

HESTER

It's all right, Mrs. Elton. Thank you.
> (MRS. ELTON *shrugs her shoulders and departs.* COLLYER *and* HESTER *still stare at each other.* HESTER's *alarm, now that she is finally confronted with her husband, seems to have dissipated.*)

COLLYER

Are you all right?

HESTER

Yes, I'm all right.

COLLYER

What happened?

HESTER

How much did that boy tell you on the telephone?

COLLYER

Enough to spare you any necessity of lying to me.

HESTER

I must be careful what I say. Attempted suicide is a crime, isn't it?

COLLYER

Yes.

HESTER

And I'm speaking to a judge.

COLLYER

You're speaking to your husband.

HESTER

Shall we say a nervous *crise?*

COLLYER

Nonsense. You're as sane a person as any in the world.

HESTER

Perhaps I've changed since I left you, Bill. No, I'd better not say that. It might give you the opportunity of saying "I told you so."

COLLYER

You misjudge me.

HESTER

Misjudge a judge. Isn't that *lèse-majesté?*

(*There is a pause while* HESTER *stares at him.*)

COLLYER

Why didn't you let me know you were in London?

HESTER

The last time I saw you you told me you never wanted to hear from me again.

COLLYER

The last time I saw you I didn't know what I was saying. How long have you been back from Canada?

41

HESTER

Oh, three or four months now. Freddy lost his job, you see
—that's to say, he gave it up—it wasn't a very good one—
and neither of us liked Ottawa very much.

COLLYER

Why didn't you answer my letter?

HESTER

I never got a letter.

COLLYER

Oh, didn't you? I addressed it to the aircraft firm in Ottawa, and put "please forward"—

HESTER

Oh. We left rather hurriedly, you see. And I—forgot to
leave a forwarding address. What did you say in the letter,
Bill?

COLLYER

Just that you could have your divorce if you still wanted it.

HESTER

Oh!

COLLYER

Not getting a reply, I'm afraid I've taken no steps—

HESTER

No. That was generous of you, Bill. Still I should have

thought what you said before about the scandal would be even more operative now that you're a judge.

COLLYER

What I said before was exaggerated. I wanted to put every difficulty in your way that I possibly could.

HESTER

Sit down, Bill, now you're here. It's nice to see you again. Have a cigarette?

COLLYER

(*Ignoring the proffered packet*)
No, thank you. (*He lights hers*) Has he deserted you?

HESTER

He's playing golf at Sunningdale. He plays there a lot, these days. I wonder you haven't run into him.

COLLYER

I haven't been to Sunningdale since—I felt too strongly.

HESTER

After all this time? Still, I suppose ten months isn't very long. I keep thinking it's so much longer.

COLLYER

Has it seemed so much longer?

HESTER
(*Quietly*)

Yes, Bill. Almost a lifetime.

(*Pause.*)

COLLYER

Is he being unfaithful to you?

HESTER

No.

COLLYER

He still loves you?

HESTER
(*After a slight pause*)

As much as he did ten months ago.

COLLYER

And you still love him?

HESTER

Yes, Bill. I still love him.

COLLYER

Is it money?

HESTER

No. It isn't money.

44

COLLYER

He's still got a job?

HESTER

Not as a test pilot. He gave that up some time ago. He's —he's working in the city now, you know.

COLLYER

In a job in which they allow him to play golf on Mondays?

HESTER

Well, it's a sort of free-lance job, you see.

COLLYER

Yes. I see. What salary—

HESTER

You're on the wrong track, Bill. All right. We do owe a month's rent, but money had nothing to do with it.

COLLYER

What was it then?

HESTER

Bill, I'm not in the witness box and you'll never get me to confess that I had any reason for trying to kill myself last night.

COLLYER

But you did try to kill yourself?

HESTER

While the balance of my mind was temporarily disturbed. Isn't that the legal phrase?

COLLYER

What was it that disturbed the balance of your mind?

HESTER

Oh dear, oh dear, I don't know. A great tidal wave of illogical emotions.

COLLYER

Can't you give a name to those emotions?

HESTER

Yes, I suppose so. Anger, hatred and shame, in about equal parts, I think.

COLLYER

Anger—at Page?

HESTER

Yes.

COLLYER

And hatred?

HESTER

Of myself, of course. (*Pause*) Shame at being alive.

COLLYER

I see.

HESTER

Do you?

COLLYER

No, I suppose I don't. Can I do anything to help?

HESTER

No, Bill. Nobody can.

COLLYER

Well, at least I've found you again.

HESTER

Were you looking so very hard?

COLLYER

No. You see, rather foolishly I thought my indifference would hurt your vanity. (HESTER *only smiles in reply*) You must understand that I'm very inexperienced in matters of this kind.

HESTER
(*Gently*)

So am I, Bill. Almost as inexperienced as yourself.

(*She touches his arm sympathetically. He takes hold of a wrist watch she is wearing.*)

COLLYER

I'm glad you still wear it.

HESTER

What? (*Remembering with an effort*) Oh yes, of course.
An anniversary present, wasn't it?

COLLYER

Our seventh.

HESTER
(*Awkwardly*)

It was a good party we gave that night. (COLLYER *nods*)
All our nicest friends were there. I read Sibyl's new book.
I didn't think it was as good as her last. Tell me, is David
very pompous now he's Solicitor-General?

COLLYER

No. Not very.

HESTER

Is Alice still as gay as ever? (COLLYER *nods*) Oh dear,
nostalgia is dangerous. I made a speech that night, didn't I?

COLLYER

Yes. Old Lord Marsden was wildly impressed.

HESTER

That's what comes of being a professor's daughter. I could
always impress your erudite friends when put to it. I only
wish I were as good with Freddy's.

COLLYER

Aren't you?

HESTER

Oh, no. On pub crawls I'm a terrible fish out of water.

COLLYER

Pub crawls?

HESTER

You needn't look so shocked, Bill. There's nothing in this world more respectable than pub crawls. More respectable or more unspeakably dreary.

(*Pause.*)

COLLYER

Hester—why?

HESTER

Why?

COLLYER

It doesn't matter. The question I was going to ask you is too big to put into a single sentence.

HESTER
(*Slowly*)

Perhaps the answer could be put into a single word.

COLLYER

We might disagree on the choice of that word.

HESTER

I don't expect so. There are polite words and impolite words. They all add up to the same emotion. (*Pointing to a picture*) That top one is my latest painting.

COLLYER

Very nice. What were you angry with Page about?

HESTER

Oh, lots of things. Always the same things.

COLLYER

What?

HESTER

That word we were talking about just now. Shall we call it love? It saves a lot of trouble.

COLLYER

You said just now his feelings for you hadn't changed.

HESTER

They haven't, Bill. They couldn't, you see. Zero minus zero is still zero.

(*Pause.*)

COLLYER

How long have you known this?

HESTER

I've known it—from the beginning.

COLLYER

But you told me—

HESTER

I don't know what I told you, Bill. If I lied, I'm sorry. You must blame my strict and conventional upbringing. You see I was brought up to think that in a case of this kind it's more proper for it to be the man who does the loving.

(*Pause.*)

COLLYER

But how, in the name of reason, could you have gone on loving a man who, by your own confession, can give you nothing in return?

HESTER

Oh, but he can give me something in return, and even does, from time to time.

COLLYER

What?

HESTER

Himself.

COLLYER
(*Stares at her*)

Perhaps you're right, Hester. Perhaps there is no one who can help you.

HESTER
(*Mockingly*)
Except myself, you were going to say.

COLLYER
Yes, I was.

HESTER
I thought you were. I think that's rather good, don't you?

(COLLYER *looks at the picture.*)

COLLYER
Yes, is it for sale?

HESTER
Oh yes, I suppose so—if anyone will buy it.

COLLYER
I'll buy it.

HESTER
(*With a hint of anger*)
No, you won't.

COLLYER
Why not?

HESTER
Because I don't want you to—that's why.

COLLYER

Hester—don't be childish. I like that picture and I'm prepared—

HESTER

Leave the subject, do you mind? I wanted your opinion, not your money—(*There is a ring on the doorbell. Calling*) Who is that?

MILLER
(*Off-stage*)

Miller.

HESTER
(*To* COLLYER)

This is the man who looked after me this morning. I'd better let him in.

(COLLYER *nods.* HESTER *opens the door.* MILLER *comes in, now dressed, but untidily.*)

MILLER

I told you to stay in bed.

HESTER

Thanks to your ministrations, Mr. Miller. I feel perfectly all right now. This is Sir William Collyer—Mr. Miller.

(*The men nod to each other.*)

MILLER
(*Turning to* HESTER)

Come down to the light and let me have a look. (*He*

examines her eyes) Tongue. (HESTER *extends her tongue.*
MILLER *feels her pulse*) Yes. You have a strong constitution.
(*With a slight smile*) You should live to a ripe old age.

HESTER
(*Matching his irony*)
Barring accidents, of course.

MILLER
Barring accidents, of course. I left a bottle in your bedroom.
May I get it?

(*He turns to go.* COLLYER *stops him.*)

HESTER
Please.

COLLYER
Mr. Miller. I'm very grateful to you for all you did for
my—for Mrs. Page—

MILLER
You needn't be, Sir William. I did very little for—Mrs.
Page.

COLLYER
(*Bristling a little*)
I take it, Mr. Miller, that you're not a qualified practitioner?

MILLER
You take it quite correctly.

COLLYER

I only ask because a qualified doctor, in a case of this rather delicate kind, is strictly bound by a certain code.

MILLER

Yes, I've heard of it. It's much the same as the English schoolboy's code, isn't it? No sneaking.

COLLYER
(*Heavily*)

I congratulate you on your knowledge of our idioms, Mr. Miller.

MILLER

I've spoken no other language since 1938, except for a year in an internment camp. Don't worry, Sir William. Or you, Mrs. Page. I won't sneak.

(*He goes into the bedroom.*)

COLLYER

I don't think I like the look of him. I'm worried.

HESTER

He looks too much like a blackmailer to be one.

COLLYER

I don't share your confidence. Damn it! We ought at least to have offered him a fee—

HESTER

He wouldn't accept it. You'd insult him—

COLLYER

I wonder. It's a fair test. (MILLER *emerges from the bedroom with a bottle in his hand*) Mr. Miller, if you were a qualified practitioner there is one other thing you would do. (MILLER *looks at* COLLYER *inquiringly.* MILLER *gives no sign of having understood.* COLLYER *takes out his wallet and pulls out a five-pound note, which he politely extends to* MILLER) Five pounds!

MILLER

(*After a pause, with a faint smile*)

Thank you. I'll send you a receipt.

(*He takes the note and goes out.* COLLYER *makes an expressive gesture at* HESTER.)

HESTER

You win.

COLLYER

The study of human nature is, after all, my profession. If you have any trouble from him, please get in touch with me at once.

HESTER

(*Wearily*)

Yes, Bill.

COLLYER

(*He looks at his watch*)

I must go. I have to be in court in fifteen minutes.

HESTER

Did you bring the car?

COLLYER

Yes.

HESTER

Still the Austin?

COLLYER

No. A new one. Or rather an older one—but a Rolls.

HESTER

Oh. I must have a look at it. (*She goes to the window and peers through. She darts back immediately*) Oh, Lord! You brought Flitton—

COLLYER

Yes.

HESTER

I wonder who he thought you were going to visit in this low neighborhood. You didn't tell him?

COLLYER

Of course not.

HESTER

How is he?

COLLYER

Very well.

HESTER

I miss him. I miss them all. Even Miss Wilson. I bet she's been pounding that typewriter with a positive paean of triumph since I left.

COLLYER

There is, perhaps a certain added flourish to her style. (*Pointing to the picture*) You know, I do like that picture —very much.

HESTER
(*She joins him at the picture*)
I'll give it to you.

(*Pause.*)

COLLYER
(*Quietly*)
What a very handsome present! Thank you. Which reminds me—many happy returns of yesterday.

HESTER

Thank you. (*Indicating the picture*) Will you take this now, or shall I send it to you?

COLLYER
(*After a slight pause*)
May I call for it?

HESTER

When?

COLLYER

What time are you expecting Page?

HESTER

Oh, not till about seven.

COLLYER

I'll come to tea.

HESTER

About five?

COLLYER

Five-twenty.

HESTER

Right.

COLLYER

Good-bye.

HESTER

Good-bye.

COLLYER

I wish you'd try to find a way I could help you.

(*Pause.*)

HESTER

I will try to find a way.
(COLLYER *smiles at her and goes.* HESTER, *left alone,*
takes a cigarette from her pocket. Then, having lit it,

*she goes to the window, concealing herself behind the
curtains, but looking out.* HESTER *sighs. Then she
goes to the sofa, lies down on it, her back to the door,
and picks up a book. After a moment she puts the
book down on her lap and stares sightlessly ahead.
The door opens and* FREDDY PAGE *comes in. He is in
his late twenties or early thirties, with a sort of boyish
good looks that do not indicate age. He carries a suitcase and a bag of golf clubs. The latter he deposits
in a corner with a rattle. It is plain that* HESTER *has
heard him come in, but she does not turn her head.
During the ensuing scene she never looks at him at
all, until the moment indicated later.*)

FREDDY

Hullo, Hes; how's tricks?

HESTER

(*At window*)

I thought you were playing golf?

FREDDY

We gave up the idea. It started to rain.

HESTER

It's not raining here.

FREDDY

Pouring down in Sunningdale.

HESTER

Well, you're up to town early—it's not ten yet.

FREDDY

Jackie Jackson gave me a lift. He's got a Jaguar. Terrific job. We did ninety-three miles an hour down the Great West Road. By the way, there was a bloody great Rolls moving off from here just as I came in. Wonder whose it was. (*He kisses her on the back of her head*) Do you know? (*He takes his golf shoes into the kitchen*) You don't suppose old Pa Elton's lashed out and invested his life savings, do you? I wouldn't be surprised, considering what he makes out of us.

HESTER

Did you have a good week-end?

FREDDY

Not bad. Won both my matches. Took five pounds off Jackie. Won a bottle of Scotch. Match bye—and bye-bye. Jackie was livid. I wanted to double the stakes, but he wouldn't hear of it.

HESTER

You can't blame him, can you? How much did you win altogether?

FREDDY

Seven.

HESTER

Could you let Mrs. Elton have some of it?

FREDDY

I thought you were going to sell those pictures. Is there any coffee left?

HESTER

I'm not now.

FREDDY

Why not?

HESTER

I've given one away.

(*She goes into the kitchen.*)

FREDDY

(*Mildly*)

That was a bloody silly thing to go and do, wasn't it?

HESTER

Yes. I suppose it was.

FREDDY

Oh, hell! All right. She can have three. I need the rest for lunch. I'm taking a South American to the Ritz! Get me, giving lunch parties at the Ritz!

HESTER

What South American?

62

FREDDY

Bloke I met at golf yesterday. Aircraft business. I got myself given the old intro to him—you know—one of England's
most famous test pilots, D.F.C. and bar, D.S.O., all the old
ex-Spitfire bull. He seemed impressed.

HESTER

So he should.

FREDDY

Funny thing about gongs, when you think what a lottery
they were. They don't mean a damn thing in war—except as
a line-shoot, but in peacetime they're quite useful.

HESTER

That's what they're for, isn't it?

FREDDY

This bloke's worth bags of dough, Hes. He's got some sort
of tie-up with Vickers over here, I think. He might fix something. Anyway he ought to be good for a touch. I say, do you
know you haven't looked at me once since I came in?

HESTER

Haven't I, Freddy?

FREDDY

Why's that?

HESTER

I can remember what you look like.

FREDDY

(*With a guilty look*)

I haven't done anything, have I?

HESTER

(*Smiling*)

No, Freddy. You haven't done anything.

FREDDY

You're not still peeved about last night, are you? You see, the blokes wanted to play again today, and if I'd let 'em down—

HESTER

That's all right.

FREDDY

You were funny on the phone, too, I remember. There wasn't any special reason you wanted me back to dinner last night, was there? (HESTER, *still not looking at him, does not reply. She gets up from the sofa, her back to him. A sudden thought strikes* FREDDY. *Explosively*) Oh, my God! (*After an embarrassed pause*) Many happy returns!

HESTER

Thank you, Freddy.

FREDDY

Blast! I remembered it on Saturday too. I was going past Barkers' and I thought, it's too late to get her a present now,

64

I'll have to find a shop open on Sunday. Cigarettes, or something. Had you arranged anything special for dinner?

HESTER

No, nothing special. Just a steak and a bottle of claret.

FREDDY

We'll have it tonight.

HESTER

Yes.

FREDDY

Come on now, Hes. I've said I'm sorry. I can't say more?

HESTER

No, Freddy.

FREDDY

Give us a shot of those gorgeous blue orbs. I haven't seen 'em for two whole days—(*He goes to her and lifts her chin*) This is me. Freddy Page. Remember?

HESTER

I remember.

(*He kisses her. Instantly she responds, with an intensity of emotion that is almost ugly. After a moment he pushes her away and smacks her playfully.*)

FREDDY

Naughty to sulk with your Freddy. Go and get dressed.
We'll have a quick one at the Belvedere to celebrate.

HESTER

That will be fun.

FREDDY

(*Putting his clubs away*)
What have you been up to over the week-end?

HESTER

Oh, nothing very much. I went to a picture.

FREDDY

Bet you didn't practice your golf.

HESTER

I did too. For all of an hour! You don't believe me, do
you? (FREDDY *shakes his head "no"*) It's true! At the end,
I was swinging like a pro. Well, a little better, anyway. When
are you going to take me with you?

FREDDY

Pretty soon!

HESTER

Are you?

66

THE DEEP BLUE SEA

FREDDY

Go and get dressed, you.

HESTER

(*At bedroom door*)

Want me to lunch with your South American?

FREDDY

No, I think better not. I can shoot him a better line without your beady eyes on me.

HESTER

They were gorgeous orbs a moment ago.

FREDDY

They get beady in company. Go on darling. Hurry.

HESTER

Yes.

FREDDY

Still love me?

HESTER

I still love you. (*She goes into bedroom leaving the door open. She is taking off her dressing gown as she speaks and hanging it up on a hook on the door*) Oh, darling, where are you going to be between five and six?

FREDDY

Nowhere special, why?

67

HESTER

Do you mind being out? I've got someone coming in I want to see alone.

FREDDY

A customer?

HESTER

Yes.

FREDDY

All right. I'll go to that new club down the road.

HESTER

(*Smiling*)

And don't get sozzled, either. Remember our dinner.

FREDDY

Shut up, you. Go on, darling, hurry.

(*She disappears, leaving the door open.* FREDDY *goes to the bedroom door and looks in the dressing gown for cigarettes. He finds a pack and a letter in* HESTER'S *pocket. He is about to replace the letter when he glances at the envelope. He raises his eyebrows, and brings the letter into the room. He lights a smoke, and opens the envelope, then begins to read.*)

HESTER

(*Off-stage*)

Oh, darling, don't forget your coffee.

THE DEEP BLUE SEA

FREDDY
(As he sits)
What? Ahh, no—I won't forget.

(He continues to read as)

The curtain falls

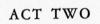

ACT TWO

ACT TWO

Scene: The same. It is now about five o'clock in the after-noon. FREDDY *is sprawling in the attitude in which we have already seen him in one armchair, while his friend,* JACKIE JACKSON, *reclines in another. There is a bottle of whisky on the table, and a siphon, and both men are holding glasses.*

FREDDY
(*In an injured tone*)
But it's too bloody silly, old boy—just because I forgot her birthday (JACKIE *makes a sympathetic sound.* FREDDY *morosely takes another gulp of whisky*) My God, if all the men who forgot their wives' birthdays were to come and find suicide notes waiting for them, the line of widowers would stretch from here to—to John o' Groats.

JACKIE
Further, old boy.

FREDDY
You can't go further.

JACKIE
Well, from here to John o' Groats and back—and ending up at the Folies Bergère.

73

FREDDY
(*Angrily*)

Shut up, Jackie. I asked you round for help and advice and not to let loose a flood of corny wisecracks.

JACKIE

Sorry, Freddy, only the way you tell it, it sounds so idiotic. Are you sure it wasn't a joke, just to scare you?

FREDDY

I've told you it wasn't. (FREDDY *has risen and is taking* JACKIE's *glass from his willing hand for replenishment*) I got the whole story out of old Ma Elton. She definitely tried to gas herself and would have succeeded if there'd been a shilling in the blasted meter—

(*He has replenished both glasses generously.*)

JACKIE

Well, that shows she couldn't have been too serious about it. (*Taking glass from* FREDDY) Oh, thanks. Cheers.

FREDDY

Where's your imagination? If you're in a state of mind where you're going to try and bump yourself off, you don't think about things like meters.

JACKIE
(*Judiciously*)

Well, I would.

FREDDY

That from the man who once wrote off three Spitfires by forgetting to put his ruddy wheels down.

JACKIE

That was different. I wasn't trying to bump myself off.

FREDDY

You gave a fairly good imitation of it—

JACKIE

(*Bridling*)

At the Court of Inquiry it was definitely established—

FREDDY

Oh, shut up, Jackie. We're talking of something a good deal more important—

JACKIE

Well, you started it. All I said was—about the meter—

FREDDY

I know what you said about the meter. But you're wrong. I've been into the whole thing, and you can take it from me that she did definitely try, last night, to kill herself.

JACKIE

And all because you forgot her birthday? But that's the sort of boner I'm always pulling on my Liz.

75

FREDDY

I know, old boy. I tell you, it knocked me ruddy flat.

JACKIE

I can imagine.

FREDDY
(*Explosively*)

My God, aren't women the end!

JACKIE
(*Nodding sympathetically*)

Where is she now?

FREDDY

Out looking for me, I shouldn't wonder.

(*He collects* JACKIE's *glass again.*)

JACKIE

No, thanks.

(FREDDY *replenishes his glass as he speaks.*)

FREDDY

She was having her bath. After I'd read that letter I ran downstairs to Ma Elton and after that I just took a powder. I had to have a drink quick, and anyway I was damned if I was going in to Hes and fall on my knees and say, my darling I have grievously sinned in forgetting your birthday; if

I promise you I'll never do it again, will you promise me you'll never gas yourself again. I mean the whole thing's too bloody idiotic—

JACKIE

There must be something else.

FREDDY

There isn't anything else.

JACKIE
(*Tentatively*)

Another girl?

FREDDY

There never has been.

JACKIE

Had a lot of rows lately?

FREDDY

No. As a matter of fact, these last few months I've been thinking we've been getting on better than before.

JACKIE
(*Evidently remembering Liz*)

There must have been some rows.

FREDDY

Very minor ones. Nothing like the real flamers we had when we first started.

JACKIE

What were they about?

FREDDY

(*Uncomfortably*)

Usual things. (JACKIE *waits for him to continue*) Damn
it, Jackie, you know me. I can't be a ruddy Romeo all the
time.

JACKIE

Who can?

FREDDY

According to her, the whole damn human race—male part
of it, anyway.

JACKIE

What does she know about it?

FREDDY

Not a damn thing. A professor's daughter, living in Ox-
ford, marries the first man who asks her and falls in love with
the first man who gives her an eye. (*After a slight pause*)
Hell, it's not that I'm not in love with her too; of course I
am. Always have been and always will, I guess. But—well—
moderation in all things—that's always been my motto. (*At
the table*) Have another. (*Pouring himself one*) I've got
nothing on my conscience in that respect. I never gave myself
that sort of a build-up with her. She knew what she was taking on.

JACKIE

You don't think it's the marriage question that's upset her?

FREDDY

No. I'm the one that gets upset by that—not her. Person-
ally, I can't wait for that divorce. All this hole-in-the-corner
stuff gets me down.

JACKIE

Well, don't you think it might be getting her down, too?

FREDDY

She jumped that fence a year ago. I was the one that
wanted to wait. She didn't. That was the first of our flamers.
(*He moodily sips his drink, lost in thought*) My God, it's so
damned unfair. Supposing she'd pulled it off last night, do
you realize what everyone would have said? That I'd bust
up a happy marriage, and then driven Hes to suicide. I'd
have been looked on as a ruddy murderer. Did she think
of that, I wonder? Who the hell would have believed what
I've just told you now?

JACKIE

(*With unconscious irony*)

Anyone who knows you.

FREDDY

Yes, but this would have been front-page stuff. All over
the ruddy *Daily Mirrors* of the world. Think of that. And this

read out in court. (*He flourishes the letter*) My God, I'd have been lucky to have got out without being lynched. The coroner would certainly have added a rider—

JACKIE

Rider? Oh, is that that thing where they say "In our opinion, Mr. Whosit is a pretty prize stinker"?

FREDDY

I was thinking at lunch today at the Ritz—I'd never have been able to go into a restaurant again, without people nudging and pointing—

JACKIE

Oh, by the way, how did that go off—your lunch with Lopez?

FREDDY

(*Savagely*)

Do you mind not changing the subject? If I'm boring you with this story, just say so and we'll have a cozy little chat about the weather.

JACKIE

I'm sorry. Only wanted to know if he'd offered you anything, that's all. Go on about Hes, then.

FREDDY

(*Muttering*)

Hell. This is really getting me down. Sorry, Jackie. Didn't mean to bite your head off.

80

JACKIE

That's all right.

FREDDY

Lopez? Yes, he offered me a job, all right.

JACKIE

Good show.

FREDDY

Test pilot in South America.

JACKIE

Oh, Lord: I don't suppose you want to go to South America.

FREDDY

I don't want to go anywhere—as a test pilot.

JACKIE

They say you were the tops.

FREDDY

I was—a year ago. Since then—things have changed a bit. (*He points to his glass*) This stuff isn't exactly what the doctor ordered, for nerve or judgment. Besides, I'm too ruddy old. You're finished in that racket at twenty-five. I wouldn't last a week. I want something chairborne—not airborne—I've had flying for life. (*He rises to get another drink*) Want one?

JACKIE

No, thanks. Do you think you ought to?

81

FREDDY

I know I ought to. Why? Am I drunk?

JACKIE

No. It's only that I gather you've been at it most of the morning.

FREDDY

And I shall be at it most of the evening too. I shall be at it until I've forgotten that this (*He indicates the letter*) ever existed.

(*He gets himself a drink and slumps back into his chair. In speech and in manner he is not drunk, but from now on he is beginning to show some of the wildness and excitability of the habitual drinker who has had about his complement.*)

JACKIE

(*Pointing to the letter in* FREDDY's *hand*)

Doesn't that give you any more clues?

FREDDY

Read it and see.

JACKIE

No. I don't think so.

FREDDY

Squeamish, aren't you?

JACKIE

Well— a thing like that—it's a bit—private, isn't it?

FREDDY

Bloody private, it would have been read out in court, by the coroner, wouldn't it?

JACKIE

There *is* that, I suppose.

FREDDY

There is that, you suppose. All right. I'm the coroner. You're the public. Now listen: (*Reading*) "My darling—a moment ago, before I took the aspirin, I knew exactly what I wanted to say to you. I have run through this letter in my mind so very often and it has always been most eloquent and noble and composed. Now—those moving, pretty words just don't seem to be there. I think it's because, this time, I know I really am going to die—"

JACKIE

Look, old boy, don't go on. Knowing Hes as I do, I'd really rather not hear the rest—

FREDDY

You're damn well going to hear the rest. I've got to read this to someone.

JACKIE

Still it's addressed to you and no one else.

FREDDY

No one else—except, of course, the readers of all the Sunday papers. Now, listen, blast you. (*Reading*) "I know that, in the morning, when you read this letter, any feelings you ever had for me, and you had some, will be driven out of your heart for ever. Poor Freddy—poor darling Freddy. I'm so sorry." Sorry? All right. Here's your clue. "You'll want to know why, and I'd so much like to make you understand, because if you understood you might forgive. But to understand what I'm doing now, you must feel even a small part of what I'm feeling now, and that I know you can never do. Just accept that it isn't your fault—it really isn't, Freddy—believe that. You can't help being as you are—I can't help being as I am. The fault lies with whichever of the gods had himself a good laugh up above by arranging for the two of us to meet— (HESTER *comes in quietly.* JACKIE *sees her and signals to* FREDDY *who does not notice*) Forgive my bad writing. I think perhaps the drug is beginning—"

HESTER

(*In a cool voice*)

Hullo, Jackie.

JACKIE

Hullo!

HESTER

How are you?

JACKIE

Very well, thanks, Hes.

84

HESTER

Where have you two been all afternoon?

JACKIE

(*Acutely embarrassed*)

I haven't been with Freddy. I was at home, and he called me. Asked me over for a chat—

HESTER

I see. (*To* FREDDY) Where were you, Freddy?

FREDDY

A lot of places.

HESTER

I've been to most of them.

FREDDY

I thought you might.

HESTER

Can I have that letter?

FREDDY

Why?

HESTER

It belongs to me.

FREDDY

There might be two views about that. It's got my name on the envelope.

HESTER

An undelivered letter belongs, I should say, to the sender.
Please?

> (HESTER *stands with her hand out, facing* FREDDY.
> *He gives her the letter. She tears it up methodically
> and throws the pieces into the wastebasket. Then she
> takes the bottle of whisky and goes over to a
> cupboard.*)

FREDDY

What are you doing?

HESTER

Tidying up.

FREDDY

That's my bottle. I won it.

> (*He takes it away from her and puts it back on the
> table.*)

HESTER
(*Lightly to Jackie*)
Did you have a good game yesterday, Jackie?

JACKIE

Yes, thanks.

HESTER

I hear Freddy beat you. He must be getting rather good.

JACKIE

Off that handicap, he is. It's a crying scandal. Look, Hes—
I really think—I ought to be dashing along.

HESTER

No, don't go, please. Freddy'll be going out in a minute or two and I expect he'd like you to go with him. (*To* FREDDY) Darling, you hadn't forgotten about being out at five, had you?

FREDDY

Yes. I had. What's the time now?

HESTER

Getting on.

(*She goes to the two pictures she has given to her husband, and takes them down from the walls.*)

FREDDY

And of course you don't want your respectable art-lover to see me in my present state.

HESTER

I don't know anything about your present state, Freddy. I told you this morning I wanted you to be out.

FREDDY

(*Pointing to the pictures which she is now holding*) I thought you'd given that away.

HESTER

I have. I'm going to wrap it up.

FREDDY

Then what are you going to sell this bloke?

HESTER
(*At door, with a bright smile*)
Whatever he wants to buy.

(*She goes out with the picture, into bedroom.*)

FREDDY
(*Derisively, at the closed door*)
Ha! Ha!

JACKIE
(*Concerned*)
Look, Freddy old boy, I do think you ought to go and talk to her. I'll disappear—

FREDDY
I've got time enough to talk to her. I've got a whole blasted lifetime to talk to her. You stay.

(*He pours himself a drink.*)

JACKIE
Well, go easy on the Scotch, old boy.

FREDDY
I've told you. I need it.

JACKIE
Look, Freddy, old boy, I don't want to be rude, but you don't think perhaps, you might be dramatizing this thing a bit too much?

FREDDY

Dramatizing? She's the one that's dramatizing. That cool, calm, collected act just now—you saw it. That's dramatizing —she enjoys that. I'm just a poor bloke who's having a couple of drinks because he's feeling ruddy miserable—

JACKIE

I don't expect she can be feeling exactly happy herself— whatever you say about her act just now.

FREDDY

I suppose if she were Liz and you were in my place, you'd smother her with tender embraces—

JACKIE

I think I'd talk to her about it. I'd ask her what the trouble was, and what I could do to put it right—

FREDDY

What the hell's the use of that? You heard that letter. Poor Freddy. You can't help being as you are. She's put her finger on it, all right. What am I supposed to do to put that little trouble right? Pretend to be something different? That'd be a lot of help, wouldn't it?

JACKIE

A few white lies—

FREDDY

Oh, don't be such a clot—a few white lies—damn it, man, talk sense. Do you think she's as easily fooled as that? You seem to see this as a sort of problem that that woman deals with in her advice column in the Daily Whatsit—a little domestic tiff that can be put right with a few kind words and a loving peck. Hes tried to kill herself last night.

JACKIE

(*Murmuring sadly*)

I'm sorry, old boy. Perhaps I'm a bit out of my depth.

FREDDY

Out of your depth? I should bloody well think you are. I'm out of my depth too, and it's a sensation I don't care for. My God, how I hate getting tangled up in other people's emotions. It's the one thing I've tried to avoid all my life, and yet it always seems to be happening to me. Always. (*After a pause*) You remember Dot during the war? I brought her down to the Squadron a couple of times.

JACKIE

Oh, yes. I liked her a lot. A load of fun—

FREDDY

A load of fun, until she started messing about with my service revolver.

JACKIE

She didn't—

FREDDY

No. She didn't hurt herself or me or anyone else. Still you can imagine the fun got a bit sour after that. And then there was—(*He stops*) It doesn't matter. Too many emotions. Far too ruddy many. I loathe 'em.

JACKIE

A sort of *homme fatal,* eh?

FREDDY

(*Quietly*)

It's not so funny, you know, Jackie. It's not so funny. Hes says I've got no feelings and perhaps she's right, but anyway I've got something inside that can get hurt—the way it's hurt now. I don't enjoy causing other people misery. I'm not a ruddy sadist. My sort never gets a hearing. We're called a lot of rude names, and nobody ever thinks we have a case. But look at it this way. Take two people "A" and "B." "A" loves "B"—"B" doesn't love "A," or at least not in the same way. He wants to, but he just can't. It's not his nature. Now "B" hasn't asked to be loved. He may be a perfectly ordinary bloke, kind, well meaning, good friend, perhaps even a good husband if he's allowed to be. But he's not allowed to be—that's my point. Demands are made on him which he just can't fulfill. If he tries, he's cheating, and cheating doesn't help anyone. Now if he's honest and doesn't try—well, then he's called a skunk and a heartless cad, and juries bring in ruddy riders. I mean—where the hell are you? (*He finishes his drink*) Come on. Let's get weaving.

(*There is a ring at the door.* FREDDY *goes to open it.* MILLER *is outside.*)

MILLER

Excuse me. Is Mrs. Page in?

FREDDY

No, not at the moment. You're Mr. Miller, aren't you?

MILLER

Yes. You are Mr. Page?

FREDDY

That's right. Come on in. I want to talk to you.

MILLER

Thank you.

FREDDY

You looked after my wife this morning, didn't you?

MILLER

Yes. I looked after Mrs. Page.

FREDDY

(*Introducing*)

This is Jackie Jackson. Mr. Miller. (*The two men nod to each other. To* MILLER) Have a drink?

MILLER

Thank you.

FREDDY

I'd like to know how much she said to you. Mrs. Elton says you were with her alone. Oh! you needn't worry about him. He knows all about it.

MILLER

She said nothing.

FREDDY

Nothing about why she did it?

MILLER

Nothing.

(FREDDY *hands him a drink.*)

FREDDY

Do you know why she did it?

MILLER

No.

FREDDY

Shall I tell you?

JACKIE
(*Interposing*)

No, Freddy—

FREDDY

She did it because I'd forgotten her birthday.

93

MILLER

Yes.

FREDDY

You don't look surprised.

MILLER

I'm not. I assumed it was something of the kind.

FREDDY

Something so trivial?

MILLER

Nothing can be called trivial that induces an operative desire to die.

FREDDY

But forgetting a birthday—

MILLER

Yes. That is trivial.

FREDDY

A joker—this bloke. All right. What's the real reason, then? What's behind this triviality?

MILLER

I don't think you need me to tell you that.

FREDDY

I'd like to hear it, anyway.

MILLER

Yourself, I should suppose.

FREDDY

Which just about makes me a ruddy murderer.

MILLER
(*Politely*)

A ruddy near-murderer.

JACKIE
(*Interposing*)

Look, I don't think you ought to say a thing like—

FREDDY

Shut up, Jackie.

JACKIE

But he doesn't know the facts—

FREDDY

The facts? What the hell do the facts matter? It's what's behind the facts that matters, isn't that so, Mr. Miller?

MILLER

Yes.

FREDDY

And what's behind the facts is me.

MILLER

I imagine so.

FREDDY

Little murdering me. (MILLER *nods*) All right, what would you do about it if you were me?

MILLER

That's a stupid question. Nature has not endowed me with the capacity for inspiring suicidal love.

FREDDY

Aren't you lucky?

MILLER

Yes, I suppose I am.

FREDDY

And what about a poor bloke who has this capacity for inspiring suicidal love—what does *he* do about it?

MILLER

Refuse to love at all, I'd say.
    (*There is a pause.* FREDDY *turns to the bottle of whisky.*)

FREDDY

Have another drink.

MILLER

Thank you.

FREDDY

My God, we've had this bottle. (*He is pouring the last few drops into* MILLER's *glass*) What you've just said is a load of tripe.

MILLER

Very possibly. As this gentleman has already pointed out, I know nothing of the facts.

FREDDY

One of the facts is that this character has no intention, at this stage in his life, of turning himself into a bloody hermit.

MILLER

No. I imagine he hasn't.

FREDDY

You're damn right, he hasn't old boy. Look, let's continue this argument down the road. The new club opens at four.

JACKIE

I really think I ought to get back, Freddy. Liz'll be wondering—

FREDDY

(*Ironically*)

Liz'll be wondering. (*Waving at* JACKIE) Portrait of a happily married man, Mr. Miller. A man who can be fairly certain of coming home and not finding his loving wife lying in front of a gas fire—

(HESTER *opens bedroom door and comes in.*)

HESTER

Oh, hullo!

(HESTER *comes in, the pictures now neatly wrapped and tied. She puts them away in a corner, without speaking.*)

MILLER

Good afternoon.

JACKIE

Just on my way, Hes.

HESTER

Must you go?

JACKIE

I must, I'm afraid. You're turning us out of the flat anyway, aren't you?

HESTER
(*Pleadingly*)

Yes. But I hoped you'd keep Freddy company.

JACKIE

I'm afraid I can't, Hes. I've got people coming in.

FREDDY

Bad luck, darling. No nurse for poor little Freddy-weddy —Unless, of course, Mr. Miller here would like to volunteer for the job.

MILLER

I'm afraid I have some work to do.

FREDDY

What sort of work? Curing other people's love problems?

MILLER

No. Sending out the latest prices for the St. Leger.

FREDDY

You a bookie?

MILLER

Yes.

FREDDY

Good Lord, I'd never have thought so. What price Make-shift?

MILLER

A hundred to seven.

FREDDY

I'll have fifty to three-ten. That's to say if you'll accept me as a client—

(MILLER *takes out a notebook and makes a note.*)

MILLER

I'll submit your name to my proprietor.

FREDDY

That's not you?

MILLER

Oh no. I'm only one of his many assistants.

JACKIE
(*At the door*)
Well, cheerio, Freddy. (*To* MILLER) Good-bye.

HESTER

Give my love to Liz.

FREDDY

You'd better not give her *my* love, Jackie. From all accounts it's pretty lethal.

JACKIE

Good-bye.

HESTER
(*To* JACKIE)
Good-bye.

(JACKIE *goes.* HESTER *waits at the door for* FREDDY. *On his way there he stops at the table, picks up the bottle and deposits it in the wastepaper basket.*)

FREDDY

Just tidying up.

(*He walks on to the door.*)

100

HESTER

(*Trying to conceal her anxiety*)

Freddy, I don't know that you should go out, you know.

FREDDY

I thought you wanted me out. Your customer—

HESTER

Well, Mrs. Elton can give him a message. He can come back some other time. Why don't you go and have a good lie down?

FREDDY

No. I'm a good boy. When I'm told to go—I go. (*He fumbles in his pockets. To* MILLER) Can you lend me a shilling? (MILLER *produces a shilling and gives it to him.* FREDDY *throws it on the table by door*) Just in case I'm late for dinner.

(*He goes out. Though drunk, his legs are, and have been through the previous scene, supporting him fairly steadily.*)

HESTER

(*Urgently*)

Do you know where he's going?

MILLER

To the new club down the road.

HESTER

Are you really working, or was that an excuse?

MILLER

I'm really working.

HESTER

Oh.

(She moves anxiously to the window.)

MILLER

He'll be happier by himself than with me, you know.

HESTER

Why do you say that?

MILLER

Because I seem to have become the embodiment of his conscience.

HESTER
(Bitterly)

His conscience? You seem to have found something in him that I've missed.

MILLER

They say the eyes of love are blind.

HESTER

They say that about the loved one's failings—not about his virtues. And my eyes aren't blind. They can see, quite well.

MILLER

Too well. (HESTER *looks at him*) To love with one's eyes open sometimes makes life very difficult.

HESTER

Even—unbearable.

MILLER

No. I said very difficult.

HESTER

I don't like him being alone.

MILLER

Very well, I shall volunteer.

HESTER

Thank you very much, Mr. Miller, I'm very grateful.

MILLER

There's no need. (*He has a canvas in his hand*) Did you paint this?

HESTER

Yes.

103

MILLER

I only ask because it doesn't seem to be at all in the style of the others.

HESTER

Oh, well, I did that when I was seventeen.

MILLER

Indeed. (*He examines it*) Interesting. Did you go to art school?

HESTER

No.

MILLER

A pity. There is a delicacy and freshness about this which is very striking.

HESTER

Hurry to Freddy, please, Mr. Miller. I'm very anxious. (*There is a ring at the door.* HESTER *goes to it and opens it.* COLLYER *is on the threshold. He comes in*) You're early.

COLLYER

I know. I came straight from court.

(COLLYER *frowns and slightly indicates* MILLER. HESTER *stops.*)

MILLER

I'm going, Sir William. I have an errand to perform for —Mrs. Page. Oh, by the way—(*He takes an envelope from his pocket and hands it to* COLLYER) I was just about to put this in the mail.

(*He goes.*)

HESTER

I ought to have asked you to phone me. Freddy came back unexpectedly and he's only just gone out. What's that? Your receipt?

(COLLYER *opens the envelope and takes out a five-pound note.*)

COLLYER

I imagine so. This is a piece of insolence. He's written on the back of my five pounds: "For quasi-professional services, received with thanks. K. Miller." (HESTER *smiles as* COLLYER *puts the note back in his case*) Yes. I suppose the laugh is on me. What was the errand he was going to perform?

HESTER

It doesn't matter. I promised you tea, didn't I?

COLLYER

Don't bother about tea. Moments are precious. I don't want you to waste them over a kettle in the kitchen. It's all right for me to stay for a few minutes, isn't it?

105

HESTER

Yes, Bill, I think so.

COLLYER

I saw Page just now—

HESTER

Oh! Did he see you?

COLLYER

No. I was in the car, just turning into this street. I put a newspaper up. He couldn't possibly have seen me. Besides, he was quite obviously drunk.

HESTER

Oh? What makes you think that?

COLLYER

His passage down the street was rather erratic.

HESTER
(*Brightly*)

I don't think it could have been Freddy you saw, Bill. He only left this flat a moment ago—

COLLYER
(*Reproachfully*)

Hester—

(*He indicates the glasses on the table.*)

HESTER

He'd been having a drink with a friend. (COLLYER *picks out of the wastepaper basket the empty bottle, whose head is showing. Angrily*) Really, Bill, even a judge can let his imagination run away with him.

(*She takes the bottle and puts it away in the kitchen.*)

COLLYER

How long has it been going on?

HESTER

How long has what been going on?

COLLYER

In the old days he hardly touched alcohol.

HESTER
(*Shortly*)

Is that so? I don't remember.

COLLYER

Of course you remember. At Sunningdale he didn't drink at all. He used to say it was bad for his judgment as a pilot.

HESTER

Very well, then, Bill. If in the last ten months Freddy's taken to drink, it's I who've driven him to it.

COLLYER
(*Quietly*)
And he who's driven you to suicide.

HESTER

No. I drove myself there.
(*Pause.*)

COLLYER

Hester, what's happened to you?

HESTER

Love, Bill, that's all—you know—that thing you read about in your beloved Jane Austen and Anthony Trollope. Love. "It droppeth as the gentle dew from heaven." No. That's wrong, isn't it? "It comforteth like sunshine after rain—"

COLLYER

Rather an unfortunate quotation. Go on with it.

HESTER

I can't. I've forgotten.

COLLYER

"Love comforteth like sunshine after rain and Lust's effect is tempest after sun."

HESTER

"Tempest after sun"? That would be very apt, wouldn't it, if that were all I felt for Freddy.

COLLYER

In sober truth, Hester, isn't it?

HESTER

Oh, God, Bill—Do you really think I can tell you the sober truth about what I feel for Freddy? I've got quite a clear mind—too clear, I was just told, but if it were only my mind that were involved, I could agree with you, that all I'm suffering from is infatuation—or obsession—or lust, or any of those impolite words. But in sober truth, Bill—in sober truth neither my mind, nor yours, nor anyone else's can begin to grasp what it is I feel for Freddy. It's all far too big and confusing to be tied up in such a neat little parcel and labeled lust. Lust isn't the whole of life. And Freddy is, you see. The whole of life—and of death, too, it seems. Put a label on that, if you can—(*She turns abruptly*) Lord! I wish Freddy hadn't drunk all the whisky.

COLLYER

Would you like to go out?

HESTER

No. I'd better stay in and await developments.

COLLYER

What developments?

HESTER

Oh, quite a large variety are apt to offer themselves when Freddy's on the rampage—

(*A pause.*)

COLLYER
(*At length*)
What made us choose Sunningdale that summer?

HESTER
It was your idea. You wanted the golf.

COLLYER
You weren't keen, I remember. You'd have preferred the sea.

HESTER
(*Absently*)
Yes.

(*Pause.*)

COLLYER
You know you never told me exactly how it first happened.

HESTER
No. I suppose I didn't. It was that day you were playing for the President's Cup.

(*While she speaks she does not look at* COLLYER. *It is almost as though she were talking to herself.*)

COLLYER
Oh yes, I remember.

HESTER

I came up to the golf club to fetch you to go on to that party at the Hendersons'. You were still out playing. Freddy was there alone. He'd been chucked for a game and was rather bad-tempered. I'd met him several times before, of course, but I'd never paid much attention to him. I didn't even think he was even particularly good-looking, and that RAF slang used to irritate me slightly, I remember. It's such an anachronism now, isn't it—as dated as gadzooks or odds my life?

COLLYER

He does it for effect, I suppose.

HESTER

No. He does it because his life stopped in 1940. He loved the Battle of Britain. Freddy's never been really happy since he left the RAF. (*After a slight pause*) Well, that day you were a long time over your game.

COLLYER

Yes, we were badly held up, I remember.

HESTER

Freddy and I sat on the verandah together for about an hour. For some reason he talked very sincerely and rather touchingly about himself—how worried he was about his future, how his life seemed to have no direction or purpose, how he envied you—the brilliant lawyer—

COLLYER

That was good of him.

HESTER

Oh, he meant it sincerely. Then quite suddenly he put his hand on my arm and murmured something very conventional, about envying you for other reasons besides your career. I laughed at him and he laughed back at me, like a guilty small boy. He said, "I really do, you know, it's not just a line. I really think you're the most attractive woman I've ever met." Something like that. I didn't really listen to the words, because anyway I knew then in that tiny moment when we were laughing together so close that I had no hope. No hope at all.

(*Pause.*)

COLLYER

It was that night that you insisted on coming up to London with me, wasn't it?

HESTER

Yes.

COLLYER

You didn't want to come back to Sunningdale the next week-end either, I remember—

HESTER

No.

COLLYER

No, I made you come. When, exactly—

HESTER

It was in September. You remember I went up to London with him to see a play?

COLLYER

But that meeting in the clubhouse was in June.

HESTER

June the twenty-fourth.

COLLYER

Well, during those two months, why didn't you talk to me about it?

HESTER

What would you have said to me if I had?

COLLYER

What I say now. That this boy you say you love is not only your junior, but is morally and intellectually a mile your inferior and has absolutely nothing in common with you whatever. That what you're suffering from is no more than an ordinary and rather sordid infatuation and that it's your plain and simple duty to exert every effort of will you're capable of in order to return to sanity at once. (HESTER *nods quietly. There is a pause*) And how would you have answered that?

HESTER

By agreeing with you, I suppose. But it wouldn't have made any difference.

COLLYER
(*At length*)

If we'd been able to have a child, how much difference would it have made?

HESTER
(*After a pause*)

Isn't reality enough to occupy us, Bill?

COLLYER

Meaning, I suppose, that it would have made no difference at all?

HESTER

That's not what I said.

(COLLYER *moodily rises.*)

COLLYER

It's fantastic to think what may have been caused by my decision to rent that damn villa.

HESTER

You mustn't distress yourself with that sort of thought, Bill. Freddy and I would have met anyway. Look, I think it's time you were going. You mustn't forget your present after all the trouble I've been to wrapping it up.

114

COLLYER
(*Ironically*)
You believe in affinities?

HESTER
(*Simply*)
I believe it was fated that Freddy and I should meet.

COLLYER
As it's turned out, a pretty evil fate.

HESTER
Well, if there are good affinities there must be evil ones too, I suppose. Here you are.

(*She goes to the parcel and picks it up. A key is suddenly turned in the door and it is thrown open, revealing* FREDDY. *He stands for a time in the doorway, looking from* COLLYER *to* HESTER. *Then he comes in and closes the door behind him. He appears to have sobered up a little.*)

FREDDY
I thought it might be. Not many people who come to this place have a big black Rolls.

HESTER
Where's Miller?

FREDDY
Miller?

HESTER

Didn't you see him at the club?

FREDDY

I never went to the club. You've got the same chauffeur, haven't you?

COLLYER

Yes.

HESTER

Bill came to see me because someone telephoned to him about my accident.

FREDDY

Yes. (*To* COLLYER) You've heard about her accident, have you?

COLLYER

Yes.

FREDDY

Did you ever forget her birthday?

COLLYER

No.

FREDDY

No. I shouldn't think you were a forgetful type. You're a judge now, aren't you?

COLLYER

Yes.

FREDDY

Still making bags of dough?

COLLYER

A certain amount.

FREDDY

Still love Hes?

HESTER

(*Sharply*)

Don't listen to him, Bill. He's drunk. Freddy, go and lie down.

FREDDY

See how I'm bullied. I bet you were never bullied like that.

HESTER

Freddy, please, try and behave yourself—

FREDDY

Am I behaving badly? I'm only asking the judge here a simple question. I'd rather like to know the answer. Still, I suppose it doesn't really matter—

(*He goes into the bedroom. We hear the key turning in the lock.*)

HESTER
(*Turns to* COLLYER)

I'm sorry, Bill.

COLLYER

That's all right.

HESTER

I think perhaps you'd better go.

COLLYER

Yes. (HESTER *is not looking at him, but at the bedroom door*) The answer to that question is yes, you know.

HESTER
(*Not having understood*)

What?

COLLYER

The question Page asked me just now. The answer is yes.

(*Pause.*)

HESTER

Bill, please don't.

COLLYER

I'm sorry. (*Indicating bedroom*) He's changed a lot. He looks quite different.

118

HESTER

He hasn't been well lately.

COLLYER

No. (*He stretches out his hand*) Well, good-bye.

HESTER

I'm sorry, Bill. I'm so sorry. Is there anything more I can say?

COLLYER

I don't think so.
> (*He smiles at her.* HESTER *kisses him suddenly on the cheek.*)

HESTER

Good-bye, Bill. (COLLYER *smiles at her again and goes.* HESTER *closes the door behind him and then goes quickly to the bedroom door. She knocks. Calling*) Freddy, let me in, darling. (*There is no answer. She knocks again*) Freddy, don't be childish. Let me in. (*There is no answer.* HESTER *walks away from the door and goes to get a cigarette. As she is lighting it* FREDDY *emerges from the bedroom. He has changed into a blue suit*) You're looking very smart. Going out somewhere?

FREDDY

Yes.

HESTER

Where?

FREDDY

To see Lopez about a job.

HESTER

Lopez?

FREDDY

The South American I had lunch with.

HESTER

Oh, yes. Of course, I'd forgotten. How did it go off?

FREDDY

It went off all right.

HESTER

Oh, good. You think you'll get the job?

FREDDY

Yes, I think so. He made a fairly definite offer. Of course it's up to his boss.

HESTER

Let's have a look at you. (*She inspects him*) Oh, darling, you might have changed your shirt.

FREDDY

Well, I hadn't a clean one.

HESTER

No. The laundry's late again. I'll wash one out for you tomorrow.

FREDDY

Yes. Does it look too bad?

HESTER

No. It'll pass. Your shoes need a cleaning.

FREDDY

Yes. I'll give them a rub.

HESTER

No. Take them off. I'll do them. (*She goes toward the kitchen*) Somehow or other you always manage to get shoe polish over you face—Lord knows how. (*She disappears into the kitchen.* FREDDY *takes his shoes off.* HESTER *comes back with shoe brushes and a tin of polish. She takes the shoes from him and begins to clean them. There is a fairly long silence*) Well, what's the job?

FREDDY

(*Muttering*)

Yes. I suppose I must tell you.

(HESTER *gives him a quick glance.*)

HESTER

Yes, Freddy. I think I'd like to know.

121

FREDDY

Look, Hes. *I've* got to talk for a bit now. It's not going to be easy, so don't interrupt, do you mind? You always could argue the hind leg off a donkey—and just when I've got things clear in my mind I don't want them muddled up again.

HESTER

I'm sorry, Freddy. I must interrupt at once. The way you've been behaving this afternoon, how could you have things clear in your mind?

FREDDY

I'm all right now, Hes. I had a cup of black coffee, and after that a bit of a walk. I know what I'm doing.

HESTER

And what are you doing, Freddy?

FREDDY

Accepting a job in South America as a test pilot.

HESTER

Test pilot? But you've said a hundred times you could never go back to that. After that crash in Canada you told me you had no nerve or judgment left.

FREDDY

They'll come back. I had too many drinks that time in Canada. You know that.

HESTER

Yes, I know that. So did the Court of Inquiry know that. Does this man Lopez know that?

FREDDY

No, of course not. He won't hear either. Don't worry about my nerve and judgment, Hes. A month or two on the wagon and I'll be the old ace again—the old dicer with death.

HESTER
(*Sharply*)

Don't use that idiotic RAF slang. (*More gently*) Do you mind? This is too important—

FREDDY

Yes. It is important.

HESTER

Whereabouts in South America?

FREDDY

Somewhere near Rio.

HESTER

I see. (*She continues to clean the shoes mechanically*) Well, when do we start?

FREDDY

We don't.

HESTER

We don't?

FREDDY

You and I don't, Hes. That's what I'm trying to tell you. I'm going alone.

HESTER
(*At length*)

Why, Freddy?

FREDDY

If I'm to stay on the wagon, I've got to be alone.

HESTER
(*In a near whisper*)

Have you?

FREDDY

Oh, hell—that's not the real reason. Listen, Hes, darling. (*There is a pause while he paces the room as if concentrating desperately on finding the words.* HESTER *watches him*) You've always said, haven't you, that I don't really love you? Well, I suppose, in your sense I don't. But what I do feel for you is a good deal stronger than I've ever felt for anybody else in my life, or ever will feel, I should think. That's why I went away with you in the first place, that's why I've stayed with you all this time, and that's why I must go away from you now.

124

HESTER

(*At length*)

That sounds rather like a prepared speech, Freddy.

FREDDY

Yes. I suppose it is a bit prepared. I worked it out on my walk. But it's still true, Hes. I'm too fond of you to let things slide. That letter was a hell of a shock. I knew often you were a bit unhappy—you often knew I was a bit down too. But I hadn't a clue how much the—difference in our feelings had been hurting you. It's asking too damn much of any bloke to go on as if nothing had happened when he knows now for a fact that he's driving the only girl he's ever loved to suicide.

HESTER

(*In a low voice*)

Do you think your leaving me will drive me away from suicide?

FREDDY

(*Simply*)

That's a risk I shall just have to take, isn't it? It's a risk both of us will have to face.

(*Pause.*)

HESTER

Freddy, you mustn't scare me like this.

FREDDY

No scare, Hes. Sorry, this is on the level.

125

HESTER

You know perfectly well you'll feel quite differently in the morning.

FREDDY

No, I won't, Hes. Not this time. (*Pause*) Besides, I don't think I'll be here in the morning.

HESTER

Where will you be?

FREDDY

I don't know. Somewhere. I think I'd better get out tonight.

HESTER

No, Freddy, no!

FREDDY

It's better that way. I'm scared of your arguing. (*Passionately*) I know this is right, you see. I know it, but with your gift of the gab, you'll muddle things up for me again, and I'll be lost.

HESTER

I won't, Freddy. I won't. I promise I won't. But you must stay tonight. Just tonight.

FREDDY
(*Unhappily*)

No, Hes.

126

HESTER

Just tonight, Freddy. Only one night.

FREDDY

No. Sorry, Hes.

HESTER

Don't be so cruel, Freddy. How can you be so cruel?

FREDDY

Hes, this is our last chance. If we miss it, we're done for. We're death to each other, you and I.

HESTER

That isn't true.

FREDDY

It is true, darling, and you've known it longer than I have. I'm such a damn fool and that's been the trouble, or I should have done this long ago. That's it, you know. It's written in great bloody letters of fire over our heads—"You and I are death to each other."

(HESTER *is unrestrainedly weeping.* FREDDY *comes over to her and picks up his shoes.*)

HESTER

I haven't finished them.

127

FREDDY

They're all right. (*He begins to put them on*) Please don't cry. You don't know what it does to me. (*He rises*) I'm sorry, Hes. My God, I'm sorry.

HESTER

Not now. Not this minute. Not this minute, Freddy? (FREDDY *finishes putting on his shoes, and then turns away from her, brushing his sleeve across his eyes. Going to him*) You've got all your things here. You've got to pack—

FREDDY

I'll send for them.

HESTER

You promised to come back for dinner.

FREDDY

I know. I'm sorry about that.
     (*He kisses her quickly and goes to the door.*)

HESTER
(*Frantically*)

But you can't break a promise like that, Freddy. You can't. Come back just for our dinner, Freddy. I won't argue, I swear, and then if you want to go away afterward—(FREDDY *goes out.* HESTER *runs to the door after him*) Don't go. Freddy, come back. Don't leave me alone tonight. Not tonight. Freddy, don't leave me alone tonight.
     (*She has followed him out as·*
          The curtain falls

ACT THREE

ACT THREE

Scene: The same. It is about eleven at night.

HESTER *is sitting in an armchair, staring toward the window. She remains in this attitude for several moments and then suddenly the telephone bell rings; she jumps to her feet and runs over to the table.*

HESTER

Hullo! Oh! No, he's not in, I'm afraid. Yes, it is. Who is that? Oh, yes! Good evening! I don't know exactly when he'll be back. What's the time now? Eleven? Is it as late as that? Oh, no! I wasn't asleep—just reading—Yes, I expect him in quite soon—It's about golf? Yes, I'll get him to ring you. He knows your number, doesn't he? Quite all right. Good night. (*There is a ring at the door.* HESTER *goes to open it.* MRS. ELTON *is outside*) Yes, Mrs. Elton?

MRS. ELTON.

Hullo, dear. Just thought I'd pop up and see how you were. (*Looking round*) Mr. Page not in?

HESTER

No.

MRS. ELTON

Don't you want the fire on? It's turned quite old all of a sudden.

131

HESTER

No, thank you.

MRS. ELTON

Fancy not drawing the curtains.

(*She does so.* ANN WELCH *puts a tentative head round the door.*)

ANN

Oh. Excuse me.

HESTER

Good evening, Mrs. Page. I just wondered if Philip was here, by any chance—

HESTER

Philip? Oh, your husband. No. Why should he be?

ANN

I thought perhaps Mr. Page was back and—

HESTER

(*Excitedly*)

Is he with him?

ANN

Yes, I think so.

HESTER

Where?

ANN

Well, I don't know. I didn't want to go with them because I had some work to do. Still, they've been gone nearly two hours now and—

HESTER
(*To* ANN)

How did you meet him?

ANN

We were having our dinner at the Belvedere—and Mr. Page was in the bar and then he came up and sat at our table.

HESTER

I see.

ANN

Of course we hardly know him at all, you know, but he was very nice and friendly and said he wanted company, and he gave us a brandy each, and then, after that, he asked Philip to go on with him to this club for a few moments.

HESTER

Which club?

ANN

I'm afraid I can't remember the name.

HESTER

How was he?

ANN

Well, do you mean was he . . .

HESTER

Drunk, yes!

ANN

I wouldn't actually say drunk. Of course that was two hours ago. Philip doesn't drink at all, of course, so that's all right. The only thing is—I know it's awfully silly of me, but I'm not very good at being left alone.

HESTER
(*With a faint smile*)
Yes, I quite understand, Mrs. Welch. Well, you mustn't worry. I expect your husband will be back very soon.

ANN

Oh, yes. I expect so. If he comes in here, send him straight up, won't you?

HESTER

I will. Good night.

(ANN *turns to go.*)

134

ANN

Good night.

(ANN *closes the door as she goes.*)

HESTER
(*Calling*)

Mrs. Elton, do you remember the name of the new club?

MRS. ELTON

No, dear. I don't, I'm afraid.

HESTER
(*Suddenly*)

I remember a card came? (*She searches little pile of cards on mantlepiece*) The Crow's Nest.

MRS. ELTON

That's right. I knew it was something like that.

(*She watches* HESTER *sympathetically as she finds the number and begins to dial.*)

HESTER

Hullo? Oh, is Mr. Page there? Page—Yes, that's right—Yes? Oh. How long ago? Half an hour. I see. Do you know where he went? No. That's all right—If he comes back will you tell him his wife called—(*Frantically*) no—waiter—don't tell him anything—anything at all—Yes, that's right. Good night.

(*She rings off.* MRS. ELTON *shakes her head.*)

MRS. ELTON

I can't understand how he could go and do a thing like that—leaving you alone tonight after what happened—

HESTER
(*Abruptly*)
Mrs. Elton, haven't you got some work to do?

MRS. ELTON
(*Quietly*)
Yes, dear. Plenty.
(*She goes to the door.*)

HESTER
I'm sorry. I didn't mean to be unkind.

MRS. ELTON
Oh, you don't need to tell me. You couldn't mean to be unkind. You're not that sort. I'll let you into a little secret. You're my favorite tenant.

HESTER
Am I?

MRS. ELTON
(*Nodding*)
Sad, isn't it, how one always seems to prefer nice people to good people, don't you think? (*She has opened the door.* MILLER, *wearing an overcoat is outside. He is carrying a rather large leather bag*) Oh, good evening, Mr. Miller. You're back from your work early?

MILLER

Yes. (*To* HESTER) How are you tonight, Mrs. Page?

HESTER

Quite well, thank you. Do you usually work as late as this?

MILLER

Sometimes.

HESTER

What have you got in that formidable-looking bag?

MILLER

It is nothing. Nothing at all.

(*He goes up the stairs.*)

MRS. ELTON

Oh, Mr. Miller, I don't like to ask you but I wonder if you'd just have a look at Mr. Elton tonight. He's bad again.

MILLER
(*Off-stage*)

I'll come down in five minutes.

MRS. ELTON

Thank you ever so much. I'm very grateful. You shouldn't have asked him that about the bag, dear. He hates to tell.

HESTER

(*Abstractedly*)

I'm sorry. I wasn't really curious. Just talking for the sake of talking.

(*She is staring at the telephone.*)

MRS. ELTON

If I were you, dear, I wouldn't use that thing again tonight.

HESTER

Perhaps you're right.

(*She sits down.*)

MRS. ELTON

Why not go to bed? I'll bring you a nice warm drink—(HESTER *shakes her head*) Or I'll get Dr. Miller to give you one of his sleeping pills—

HESTER

He *is* a doctor, of course, isn't he?

MRS. ELTON

Well. He was.

HESTER

I see. I knew he'd been in trouble.

MRS. ELTON

How, dear?

HESTER

Fellow-feeling, I suppose.

MRS. ELTON

Yes, he *was* in trouble once. Bad trouble (HESTER *nods*) Don't say I told you, will you? Poor Mr. Miller! I'm sorry for him. So ashamed of people knowing—

HESTER

Did he tell you about it?

MRS. ELTON

No, dear, but it was just after he'd come here there was a letter for him addressed to Kurt Muller, M.D.—and then of course I remember the case, because there'd been quite a lot in the papers about it. He must have come straight here from prison, because it was at least a year they gave him, I'm sure. Oh, I think it's a wicked shame the way they've treated him. Imagine a man like that being a bookie. There's waste for you, if you like.

HESTER

Why did he take the job?

MRS. ELTON

Because beggars can't be choosers, dear, and if a patient of his that was a bookie takes pity on him—well, he's got to eat, hasn't he? Anyway I can tell you what's in that bag if you really want to know. He goes and works every night in a hospital for infantile paralysis—unpaid, of course. That was his specialty before—apparently he was working on some sort of treatment—

HESTER

Won't he ever get back on the Medical Register?

MRS. ELTON

Oh, no. Not a hope, I should say, dear. You know what they're like, and what he did, wasn't—well—the sort of thing people forgive very easily. Ordinary normal people, I mean.

HESTER

You've forgiven it, Mrs. Elton.

MRS. ELTON

Oh, well, I see far too much of life in this place to get upset by that sort of thing. It takes all sorts to make a world, after all—doesn't it? There was a couple once in number eleven—(*She stops suddenly*) I can hear him on the stairs. (*She opens the door.* MILLER *is descending the stairs*) I'll go down and get Mr. Elton ready, shall I?

MILLER

Yes.

MRS. ELTON

I wonder if you'd be kind enough to give Mrs. Page one of your sleeping pills.

MILLER

I'd thought of that myself.

MRS. ELTON

Good. (*To* HESTER) Well, good night, dear. If you want anything just give me a ring. I'll be up with Mr. Elton most of the night anyway.

HESTER

Good night, Mrs. Elton. (*She goes.* MILLER *comes into the room, takes a bottle from his pocket, and shakes out two pills which he hands to* HESTER) Thank you, Doctor.

MILLER

I've asked you before not to call me that.

HESTER

I keep forgetting. I'm sorry.

MILLER

Are you going to bed now?

HESTER

In a moment.

MILLER
(*Turning to go*)

Don't let that moment be too long.

HESTER

Everyone is very solicitous of me this evening.

MILLER

Are you surprised? Voices carry on the stairs of this house.

HESTER

Freddy's and mine? (MILLER *nods*) Everyone heard us, I suppose. All the respectable tenants nudging each other and saying there's that woman's drunken boy friend walking out on her. Serve her right.

MILLER

I didn't say that. But then, of course, I may not be a respectable tenant.

HESTER
(*Simply*)

What should I do?

MILLER

What makes you think I can tell you?

HESTER

How near did *you* come to turning on the gas fire, once? (*Pause.*)

MILLER
(*Violently*)

Mrs. Elton, eh?

142

HESTER

You mustn't be angry with her. She's your friend. Besides, why should you mind *my* knowing? Am I such a respectable tenant?

MILLER

(*Abruptly*)

You ask my advice. Take those pills and sleep tonight, in the morning—go on living.

(*There is a ring at the door.* HESTER *opens it.* COLLYER *is outside, dressed in a dinner jacket.*)

HESTER

Bill—

COLLYER

I don't apologize. I've got to see you—

(*He comes in, glancing at* MILLER *as he does so. He nods to him.*)

MILLER

(*To* HESTER)

Yes. That is the most specific advice I can give you, I'm afraid. Good night.

(*He goes out.* COLLYER *silently hands her an opened letter which he has been holding in his hand.* HESTER *draws in her breath sharply as she sees the hand-writing. She reads it through quickly.*)

143

HESTER

When did it come?

COLLYER

I don't know. It was found about twenty minutes ago. I gather he dropped it in the box without ringing the bell. It *is* true, I suppose?

HESTER
(*Wearily*)

Yes. It's true.

(*She hands the letter back.*)

COLLYER

When?

HESTER

This afternoon. Just after you'd left.

COLLYER

What was the reason?

HESTER

What happened last night. That's why he was drunk this afternoon. He said we were death to each other—

COLLYER

In vino veritas.

144

HESTER

He wasn't so drunk when he said that.

COLLYER

Then he has more perception than I gave him credit for. What's he going to do?

HESTER

He's taken a job as a test pilot in South America.

COLLYER

I see. (*Glancing at the letter*) I rather like the phrase: "Sorry to have caused so much bother." It has a nice ring of R.A.F. understatement—(*He tears it up and throws it into the wastepaper basket*) I'm awfully sorry for you, Hester.

HESTER
(*Her back to him*)

That's all right. It was bound to happen one day, I suppose.

COLLYER

I have a faint inkling of how you must be feeling at this moment.

HESTER
(*Hard and bright*)

Oh, I'll get over it, I imagine. You're looking very smart. Where have you been?

COLLYER

At home. I had some people in to dinner.

HESTER

Oh, who?

COLLYER

Olive, the Ridgefields, an American judge and his wife—

HESTER

Was Olive in good form?

COLLYER

Fairly. She said one very funny thing.

HESTER

What was it?

COLLYER

Damn, I've forgotten. No, no, no! I remember. Now I come to think of it, it's not all that funny. It must have been the way she said it. She told the American judge he had a face like an angry cupid—

HESTER

An angry cupid? I can just hear her—(*She starts to laugh, and then continues longer than the joke appears to warrant*) An angry cupid! (*The laugh suddenly turns into sobs, desperately but unsuccessfully trying to control her emotion.*

COLLYER *sits beside her.*)

COLLYER

Hester, please. If only I could say something that would help. (HESTER *is succeeding now in recovering herself*) I know it's small comfort to you at this moment, but this must be for the best. You yourself spoke of an evil affinity, didn't you?

(HESTER, *wiping her eyes, does not reply.* COLLYER *looks around the room.*)

HESTER

I'm awfully sorry, Bill. I couldn't help it—

COLLYER

You must get out of this flat as soon as possible. In fact, I don't think you should be left alone in it at all.

HESTER

I'll be all right.

COLLYER

I'm not so sure. I think you'd better leave here tonight.

HESTER

Tonight?

COLLYER

You were alone here last night. weren't you?

HESTER

Where could I go?

COLLYER

Well, I could make a very tentative suggestion—in fact it's the suggestion that Page makes in that letter.

HESTER

No, Bill.

COLLYER

Why? Have you forgotten what I told you this afternoon?

HESTER
(*Her voice rising*)
Stop it, Bill—please. (*He is silenced by the note of strain in her voice. She gets up, a little unsteadily and goes to a cupboard*) I expect you'd like a drink, wouldn't you?

COLLYER

A good idea.

HESTER

Oh, dear! I'd forgotten that Freddy had finished the whisky.

COLLYER

It doesn't matter.

HESTER

Wait a moment. Here's something. (*She brings out a bottle of wine*) Claret. I'm afraid I uncorked it last night. It's from the local grocer. I don't know what your fastidious palate will make of it.

148

COLLYER

I'm sure it's delicious. (*He opens the bottle. She gives him two glasses. He fills them*) Well? What shall the toast be?

HESTER

The future, I suppose.

COLLYER

May I say *our* future?

HESTER
(*Gravely*)

No, Bill. Just the future. (*They drink in silence*) Is it all right?

COLLYER

Very good. (*After another pause*) And what's the future to be?

HESTER

I haven't thought yet.

COLLYER

Don't you think you should?

HESTER

I'll stay on here until I can find somewhere else. I'll try and take a studio, if I can—then I'll be able to work harder. If I can't sell my paintings, I'll get a job—

149

COLLYER

What sort of job?

HESTER

There must be something I can do.

COLLYER

(*Quietly*)

And you contemplate living alone for the rest of your life?

HESTER

I don't contemplate anything, Bill. I'm not exactly in a contemplative mood.

COLLYER

When you are, I'd like you to contemplate a very different future—

HESTER

(*Angrily*)

Bill, please, I've asked you—

COLLYER

(*Equally angrily*)

Hester, for God's sake, don't you realize what I'm offering you?

HESTER

And don't *you* realize how difficult for me it is to refuse?

150

COLLYER

Then why do you refuse?

HESTER

Because I must. I can't go back to you as your wife, Bill, because I no longer am your wife. We can't wipe out this last year as if it had never happened. Don't you understand that?

COLLYER

I only understand that I'm even more in love with you now than I was on our wedding day.

HESTER
(*Quietly*)

You weren't in love with me on our wedding day, Bill. You aren't in love with me now, and you never have been.

COLLYER

Hester!

HESTER

I'm simply a prized possession that has now got a little more prized for having been stolen, that's all.

COLLYER
(*Hurt*)

What are you saying?

HESTER

(*Upset*)

Bill, you force me to say these things. Do you think I enjoy hurting you, of all people? Perhaps we can talk some other time, when we both feel calmer.

COLLYER

We must talk now. You say I wasn't in love with you when I married you?

HESTER

I know you weren't.

COLLYER

Then why do you suppose I married you? What else did you have to offer me?

HESTER

(*Interrupting*)

I know, Bill, I know. You don't need to remind me of what a bad match I was. I was always only too conscious of it. Oh, I'm not denying you married me for love. For your idea of love. And so did I, for my idea. The trouble is they weren't the same ideas. You see, Bill, I had more to give you —far more—than you ever wanted from me.

COLLYER

How can you say that? You know I wanted your love.

HESTER

No, Bill. Not my love. You were *embarrassed by that.* You wanted me simply to be a loving wife. There's all the difference in the world.

COLLYER

Do you think I believed that story just now about a studio, or a job? Do you think I don't know exactly how you visualize your future? (HESTER *remains silent*) If you send me away now, you're lost. (HESTER *still remains silent. In a quieter voice:*) Hester, my darling, you can say what you like about my feelings for you but I'm offering you your only chance of life. Why can't you accept? It worked quite happily—once.

HESTER

Yes, it did.

COLLYER

Well, then—
(*He kisses her, but there is no response.*)

HESTER

You see, Bill, I'm not any longer the same person. You'd better go. I'll be all right.

(*Pause.* COLLYER *turns slowly and collects his hat.*)

COLLYER

You'll still want your divorce then?

HESTER

Yes, Bill, I think it would be best.

COLLYER

There'll be a lot to discuss now—business things.

HESTER

Yes. I suppose there will.

COLLYER

At the moment, are you really all right for money?

HESTER

Yes, Bill, thank you—perfectly all right.

COLLYER

Good-bye, then.

HESTER

Good-bye. (*He looks at her for quite a time, as if turning several things over in his mind that he would like to say. Then he turns his back abruptly and goes out.* HESTER *makes the slightest gesture—unseen by him—as if to restrain him, then stands staring at the closed door. She goes across to the window and through the drawn curtains watches him go out. A key is gently pushed into the lock and turned, and* PHILIP WELCH *opens the door. He looks nervously round the apparently empty room, and comes furtively in.* HESTER *appears and sees him at once. She stops dead*) Freddy—

154

PHILIP

Oh.

HESTER

How did you get in?

PHILIP

It's Page—You see, he lent me a key—He wanted me to pick up his suitcase. He's got all his shaving things in it, apparently, and says he needs them for tonight.

HESTER

Where's he going tonight?

PHILIP
(*Uncomfortably*)

I don't know.

HESTER

Where is he now?

PHILIP

Er—I don't know what the place is called.

HESTER

Where is it?

PHILIP

Somewhere in the West End.

HESTER

Greek Street?

PHILIP
(*Stubbornly*)

I don't know.

HESTER

I see. How long have you been with him?

PHILIP

Since nine.

HESTER

And he can do a lot of talking in three hours—especially when he's drunk.

PHILIP

He's not drunk. At least what he says makes sense.

HESTER

Does it?

PHILIP
(*In slightly avuncular tones*)

Lady Collyer—may I say something? Page has been very frank with me, very frank indeed—although I didn't invite his confidence—I know the whole situation, and I do understand what you must be feeling at this moment—

156

HESTER
(*Slightly amused*)

Do you, Mr. Welch?

PHILIP

I've been in love too, you know. In fact about a year ago I nearly had a bust-up in *my* marriage—over a sort of infatuation I had for a girl—quite the wrong sort of type, really, and it would have been disastrous—but I do know what it means to have to give someone up whom you—think you love. Look—do you think this is awfully impertinent of me?

HESTER

Not at all.

(HESTER, *with a faint smile, shakes her head.*)

PHILIP
(*Emboldened*)

Well, I do think you ought to—sort of—try and steel yourself to what I'm quite sure is the best course for both of you. Gosh, I know how hard it is, but I do remember, with this girl—she was an actress you know, although she wasn't well known or anything—I just sat down all alone one day and said to myself—look, on the physical side, she's everything in the world you want. On the other side—what is she? Nothing. So what I did was to write her a letter—and then I went away for a fortnight all by myself—and of course I had hell, but gradually things got sort of clearer in my mind, and when I got back I was out of the wood.

HESTER

I'm so glad.

PHILIP

Of course I think for you some place like Italy or the South of France would be better.

HESTER

Why better than Lyme Regis?

PHILIP

I know that if you were to go away and think things out honestly, Lady Collyer, you'll see how awfully petty the whole thing really is—when you get it in perspective. I mean, without trying to be preachy or anything, it *is* really the spiritual values that count in this life, isn't it? I mean the physical side is really awfully unimportant—objectively speaking, don't you think?

HESTER

(*Gravely*)

Objectively speaking. Well, it's very kind of you, Mr. Welch, to give me this advice. I'm very grateful.

PHILIP

Oh, that's all right. I'm glad you didn't fly at me for it. You see Page has been telling me about it all, and I was really awfully interested, because a thing like this, it's—well —it throws a sort of light on human nature, really.

HESTER

Yes. I suppose it does.

PHILIP

Well, may I have the bag now, please?

HESTER

It's just in through that door. (*He gets it*) Where did Freddy tell you to take that bag? To a station or somewhere, or back to the White Angel?

PHILIP

Back to the White Angel—(*Pause. Lamely*) Back to where he is.

HESTER

(*Quietly*)

Would you mind putting the bag down there and going now.

PHILIP

I'm afraid I can't do that. I promised him I'd bring it to him, you see. Well, good-bye.

(*He turns toward the door.* HESTER *is there before him and quickly turns a key in the lock. She removes the key and puts it in her pocket, as she goes toward the telephone, where she turns up a telephone book.*)

HESTER

I'm sorry for that melodramatic gesture, but I've got to detain you for a moment or two, I'm afraid. I won't keep you

159

long. There's the remains of a bottle of claret there, if you'd like it.

PHILIP

No, thank you.
(*He takes out his Yale key.*)

HESTER

I'm afraid that key's no use—they're separate locks.

PHILIP
(*Stiffly*)
Look, I really do think—

HESTER

Sit down, Mr. Welch. You've a splendid chance now of resuming your study of human nature. (*She is dialing a number.* PHILIP *stands watching her*) Hullo—I want to speak to Mr. Page—(*Louder*) Page—Oh, he is? Mrs. Jackson—No, Jackson—Yes. (*To* PHILIP) There's an awful lot of noise in there. Hullo? Darling, it's Hester—don't ring off. No scene, I promise—I promise, I promise. I just wanted to know about the job—(*Louder*) The job—Did you see the man? Oh, good—Oh, good—Well done. I see. How soon? As soon as that? Oh, Freddy—No, I'm sorry. It was just hearing you say it like that—(*Louder*) It was just hearing you say it—Look, darling, your messenger is here for your bag—only it hasn't got half of what you want for three days. Where are you going until you leave? No, don't tell me, if you don't want to. I only meant country or town? Now, let's think. You've got your flannels in the bag, so you'll just want your tweed coat—All right. What did you want done with the rest of your things? Oh, when did you post it? I'll get it tomorrow then—The cloakroom at Charing Cross—I see—Yes. I'll do that—Look, Freddy, there's one last thing I wanted you to do for me—I said there was one last thing I wanted you to do. Come and collect your bag yourself—Just to say goodbye, that's all. No. I won't, I won't. I promise I won't. I swear to you, on my most sacred solemn word of honor, I won't try and make you stay. I won't even talk, if you don't want me to. You can just take your bag and go—Freddy, trust me, trust me, for pity's sake—Freddy, don't ring off—don't—

(*She looks blankly at the receiver, and then replaces it. She stares at it a moment, evidently wondering whether to dial again, and then decides it would be useless. She goes slowly to the door, puts the key in the lock and unlocks it, indicating to* PHILIP *with a gesture that he is free to go.*)

PHILIP

Well—good night.

HESTER

Good night, Mr. Welch. Oh, by the way, your wife is rather worried about you. Perhaps you'd better slip up and see her before you go out again.

PHILIP

Yes. I will. (*Earnestly*) I'm awfully sorry—really I am.

161

HESTER

Thank you.

PHILIP

I think he ought to have come to fetch his things himself.

HESTER

So do I.

PHILIP

Although of course I understood him not wanting to come round when he thought you might try and stop him, but—still—after you gave him your sacred, solemn word of honor just now—

> (HESTER *has not previously been looking at* PHILIP. *She now turns slowly to face him.*)

HESTER

It might add a little to your appreciation of spiritual values, Mr. Welch, if I told you that I hadn't the smallest intention of keeping my sacred solemn word of honor. If Freddy had come here tonight, I would have used every trick in the book to make him stay. Of course he knew that perfectly well, and that's why he wouldn't come. (PHILIP, *shocked, stares at her in silence.* HESTER *looks up at him*) You've got exactly the same expression on your face that my father would have had if I'd said that to him. He believed in spiritual values, too, you know—and the pettiness of the physical side—Take the bag to Freddy now. Have you got enough money for a taxi?

PHILIP

Yes, thank you. (*At the door*) Can I—should I give Page any sort of message from you or anything?

(*Pause.*)

HESTER
(*Quietly*)

Just my love.

> (PHILIP *goes.* HESTER *goes to window, shuts it, locks it and pulls curtains. Then searches her handbag, on the sofa, for a shilling. There isn't one. She gets a shilling from the telephone table where Freddy had thrown it in Act Two. She puts it in the gas meter and hears it drop. Now she locks the door and puts the rug on the floor to stop the air getting in. Next she takes one of the claret glasses into kitchen and comes back with it full of water. She picks up the aspirin bottle on the table. It is empty. She takes the two tablets that* MILLER *gave her earlier in the Act out of her pocket. She is about to take them when there is a knock on the door, followed by the rattling of the door handle.*)

HESTER
(*Impatiently*)

Who is it?

MILLER
(*Off-stage*)

Open the door.

HESTER

I'm just going to bed. What do you want?

MILLER
(*Off-stage*)

I want to see you.

HESTER

Won't it keep to the morning?

MILLER
(*Off-stage*)

No.

(HESTER *impatiently goes to the door, pulls the rug up and throws it on to the sofa where it falls to the floor. She unlocks the door and lets* MILLER *in.*)

MILLER
(*Indicating key*)

Determined not to be disturbed?

HESTER

I usually lock my door at night.

MILLER

It's lucky you didn't last night.

HESTER
(*Indicating the glass of water*)

I was just going to take your pills.

MILLER

So I see.

HESTER

Do you think they're strong enough, Doctor? Could you let me have another two or three in case they don't work? (MILLER, *without replying, picks up the rug from the floor and puts it on the sofa. Then, watched by* HESTER, *he strolls to the gas fire and with a casual flick of his foot, kicks on the tap. He kicks it off*) I said could you let me have—

MILLER

I heard you. The answer is no.

HESTER

Why not?

MILLER

I've been involved enough with the police. I don't want to be accused now of giving drugs to a suicidal patient. (*He holds out his hand*) I want those pills back, please.

HESTER

Why?

MILLER

If you put a rug down in front of a door, it's wiser to do it when the lights are out.

165

HESTER

(*Angrily*)

Why are you spying on me? Why can't you leave me alone?

MILLER

I'm not trying to decide for you whether you live or die. That choice is yours—and you have quite enough courage to make it for yourself.

HESTER

(*Bitterly*)

Courage?

MILLER

Oh, yes! Courage! It takes courage to condemn yourself to death.

HESTER

That's not true!

MILLER

Most suicides die to escape. *You're* dying because you feel unworthy to live. Isn't that true?

HESTER

(*Wildly*)

How do I know what's true? I only know that I can't face life any more.

MILLER

What is there so hard about facing life? Most people seem to be able to manage it.

HESTER

How can I live without hope?

MILLER

To live without hope can mean to live without despair.

HESTER

Those are only words.

MILLER

Words can help if your mind can only grasp them. Your Freddy has left you. He's never going to come back again— never in the world—never.

HESTER

I know. I know. That's what I can't face.

(*She falls on her knees onto end of sofa.*)

MILLER

Yes you can. That word "never." Face that and you can face life. Get beyond hope. It's your only chance.

HESTER

What is there beyond hope?

MILLER

Life. You must believe that. It's true. I know.

HESTER

You can still find some purpose in living. You have your work at the hospital.

MILLER

For me the only purpose in life is to live it. My work at the hospital is a help for me in that. That is all—If you looked perhaps you might also find some help for yourself.

HESTER

What help?

(*He makes a gesture toward the paintings.*)

MILLER

Haven't you your work, too?

HESTER

Oh, that! There's no escape for me through that.

MILLER

You can make one, perhaps. There is always an escape through work.

HESTER

Not bad work.

MILLER

Yes, even bad work. Besides, you know, I'd like to buy that. (HESTER *goes across to the picture and takes it down. She hands it to him*) How much?

HESTER

It's a gift.

(He has pulled out his wallet and removes two one-pound notes. MILLER *puts the notes on the table.)*

MILLER

Look, I'm going to put these notes down here. It's what I can afford to give you—not what I think the picture's worth. If you're determined not to sell it, slip the note into an envelope and address it to me. I shall understand, and be sorry. Good night.

HESTER

Good night, Doctor.

MILLER

Not doctor, please.

HESTER

Good night, my friend.

MILLER

I could wish that you meant that. It might be that my need for friends was as great as yours.

HESTER

What makes you so sure that I don't mean it?

MILLER

I hope that I may be given a proof that you do by tomorrow morning. Surely I would have a right to feel sad if I were to lose a new-found friend—especially one whom I so much like and respect.

HESTER

Respect?

MILLER

Yes, respect.

HESTER

Please don't be too kind.

(*He approaches her quickly and takes her shoulders.*)

MILLER

Listen to me. To see yourself as the world sees you may be very brave, but it can also be very foolish. Why should you accept the world's view of you as a weak-willed neurotic better dead than alive? What right have they to judge? To judge you they must have the capacity to feel as you feel. And who has? One in a thousand? You alone know how you have felt. And you alone know how unequal the battle has always been that your will has had to fight.

HESTER

"I tried to be good, and failed." Isn't that the excuse that all criminals make?

MILLER

When they make it justly, it's a just excuse.

HESTER

Does it let them escape their sentence?

MILLER

Yes, if the judge is fair—and not blind with hatred for the criminal—as you are for yourself.

HESTER

If you could find me one extenuating circumstance—one single reason why I should respect myself—even a little.

(*The door opens and* FREDDY *appears on the threshold.*)

FREDDY

Hullo.

HESTER

Hullo.

MILLER
(*To* HESTER)

That reason you must find for yourself.

(*He goes.*)

FREDDY

He seems quite a good bloke, old Miller.

171

HESTER

Yes. He does. Come in, Freddy. Don't stand in the door. (FREDDY *shuffles in*) How are you feeling now?

FREDDY

All right.

HESTER

Thank you for coming.

FREDDY

That's O.K. I shouldn't have sent the kid anyway, I suppose.

HESTER

Had any food?

FREDDY

Yes. I had a bite at the Belvedere. What about you?

HESTER

Oh, I'll get myself something later. (*There is a pause, while* FREDDY *still watches her apprehensively*) When exactly are you off to Rio?

FREDDY

Thursday. I told you.

HESTER

Oh, yes, of course. By boat?

FREDDY

Oh, no. Flying.

HESTER

Oh, yes.

FREDDY

Oh, by the way—About the rent—those clubs'll fetch thirty or forty quid. They'll take care of old Ma Elton and the few odd bills.

HESTER

Won't you need them?

FREDDY

No. I can't fly them.

HESTER

I'll pack the rest of your things tonight and get them round to Charing Cross in the morning.

FREDDY

There's no hurry. (*Another pause*) I dropped a note in at Bill's house. He'll probably be round.

HESTER

He's been round.

FREDDY

Oh. Are you—?

HESTER

No.

FREDDY

I'm sorry.

HESTER

It's all right. It wouldn't have worked.

FREDDY

No, I suppose not. I didn't know. You'll go on with your painting, will you?

HESTER

Yes. I think so. As a matter of fact, I might even go to an art school, and start from the beginning again.

FREDDY

It's never too late to begin again. Isn't that what they say?

HESTER

Yes. They do.

(*There is a long pause.* FREDDY *seems to be waiting for* HESTER *to say something, but she stands quite still, looking at him.*)

174

FREDDY
(*At length*)
Well—

HESTER
(*In a clear calm voice*)
Well, good-bye, Freddy.

FREDDY
Good-bye, Hes. (*He moves to the door.* HESTER *still does not move.* FREDDY *turns, waiting for her to say something. She does not. He suddenly walks up to her and embraces her*) I wish I knew what the hell I was going to do without you.

> (*He kisses her. She accepts the embrace without in any way returning it. After a moment,* FREDDY *releases her, goes quickly to the door and turns around. He goes out, closing the door.*)
> (HESTER *stands quite still for a second. She looks around the room. Then she goes to the coat hooks and takes down Freddy's clothes. She brings them and piles them on the sofa. She reaches down a suitcase off a shelf. Then lights the gas fire. After lingering at the fire for a moment, she returns to Freddy's clothes and continues to pack.*)

Curtain